Piano & Keyboard Made Easy

GLOBAL
PUBLISHING
GROUP

Global Publishing Group
Australia • New Zealand • Singapore • America • London

Praise for the author

"I have known Chris Lavery for over a decade and in this time Chris has continued to be a key role model and positive influencer in my life. The life lessons he has imparted either directly to me or indirectly by my observations of his life, truly continue to shape my very thoughts, choices, observations and thereby my habits on a daily basis.

Chris has always been a shining example of learning by doing. He has on regular occasion entertained, impressed, and inspired me with his self-appointed duty of care, creativity, generosity and what can be at best described as his 'joie de vivre'. My career success as a performing artist, business owner and entrepreneur today, I can in great clarity, directly attribute to Chris' encouraging words and personal investments towards my own continued personal growth. The reason I am leading the successful life I am today as a father of two, husband and full-time creative artist, is due to the fact – in no small amount – that Chris showed me that it was all possible by being all these things himself.

That is what he does best. He demonstrates what can be achieved, who you can be and what you can do and what can be learned by anyone who wants to learn it. I don't think he can help it! If Chris himself learns something new, he will be the first one to want to show you how you can too can learn this new thing too!

I have watched him teach himself all sorts of new skills, from IT, art and fire twirling to, of course, his passion for music. I have literally seen with my own eyes (and more importantly, heard with my own ears!) his progression of learning music and the keyboard. It's clear to me that Chris has added a new string to his bow and was able to do this in such a short time, so I know this won't be something that Chris will want to keep to himself but rather share with whoever wants to learn how to do this too. That is his true nature and spirit. Chris is a generous soul who is keenly interested in bringing joy to other people's lives. If you are ready to learn – Chris has been waiting to teach you..."

– Daniel Tusia, Director Applause Entertainment

"Chris is a multi-talented entertainer and trainer with whom I have worked for three years. He is a fine singer and keyboardist; he also has the rather rare ability to communicate complex musical ideas in a very simple easy-to-understand way.

He has specially wanted to help people learn how to play the keyboards easily and has explained to me some great ideas on how to do so.

So this book is long overdue and I believe it will be very useful to those of us who want to play the keyboard but don't have the time to go through the long hours of doing it in the conventional way..."

– Eddie Moses Musician/Vocalist

"I have known and worked with Christopher for over 20 years and have always marvelled at this range of talents and skills. He is not one to let the grass grow under his feet and is constantly adding new strings to his bow. I have watched his skills on the piano grow; he didn't play at all when I first met him, and have witnessed him go from novice at the age of 40 to playing and singing to audiences a few short years later. His clarity and understanding deliver a simple easy to understand method for learning the piano. If anyone can find an easy way it is Christopher. I have no doubt that you will love his book..."

– Gabrielle Parbo, Musician/Vocalist

"Having attended one of Chris' workshops I was struck by how he took the complexities of music, simplified them and then communicated them in a way that everyone could understand.

I witnessed many people have real breakthroughs in their grasp of the theory and in their practice. And I personally came to appreciate many aspects of playing that till then had escaped me."

– Ron Gallagher, Director Funbiz

"I have known Chris Lavery for over 20 years. I first met him when, as an accomplished juggler, stilt-walker and all round circus performer, he decided he wanted to become cabaret artist – something totally out of his comfort zone. He researched what was involved and within a few months was successfully appearing in shows as a compere and singer.

Years later when Chris told me he had taken up piano I was not surprised to see how he approached his new activity. As a musician, singer and teacher myself, I am only too aware of how difficult it is for mature-aged brains to take up the challenge of playing this wonderful instrument but Chris took on the project with a totally different viewpoint. He examined the patterns and rhythms that are involved in music and combined this with his general philosophy for success – practice, persistence and patience.

Be prepared to look at things differently, try a new way, break down the rules and just give it a go – don't be afraid to start again tomorrow... Not only will this book help you understand the process of learning an instrument, I believe you stand to learn many more skills to help you in your daily life..."

– Jenny Wilkinson,
Director Hey Dee Ho Educational Services PL

"Christopher Lavery possesses the essential ingredients for success: boundless enthusiasm, a can-do spirit and a commitment to lifelong learning. He's also one of those fellows you'd love to have around to rave to, at a party at 1 am..."

– Leo Dale – Music and Video Producer

"Chris Lavery is one of a kind! He has a unique combination of showmanship, personality and talent that makes for a great entertainer, and he is a really good bloke as well. We have played music together in a band for about four years, with Chris on keys and lead vocals, and I enjoyed every minute. Chris has a great feel for music and natural showmanship. Always positive and supportive, it was Chris who encouraged me to try singing. With his tips on technique and showmanship I discovered a skill I never knew I had..."

– Nick Moody Guitarist/Vocalist

Piano & Keyboard Made Easy
Shortcuts for Learning Piano & Sounding Good Instantly
Christopher Lavery

DISCLAIMER

All the information, techniques, skills and concepts contained within this publication are of the nature of general comment only and are not in any way recommended as individual advice. The intent is to offer a variety of information to provide a wider range of choices now and in the future, recognising that we all have widely diverse circumstances and viewpoints. Should any reader choose to make use of the information contained herein, this is their decision, and the contributors (and their companies), authors and publishers do not assume any responsibilities whatsoever under any condition or circumstances. It is recommended that the reader obtain their own independent advice.

First Edition 2017

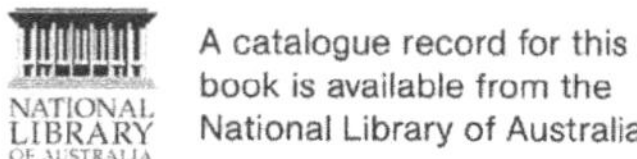

A catalogue record for this
book is available from the
National Library of Australia

Published by Global Publishing Group
PO Box 517 Mt Evelyn, Victoria 3796 Australia
Email info@GlobalPublishingGroup.com.au

Printed in China

For further information about orders:
Phone: +61 3 9739 4686 or Fax +61 3 8648 6871

To my best friend, my lover and my wife Natascha who inspires me to be my best, to see the best in others and to always strive for joy.

Thank you for investing in this book!

As a special gift to my readers, I am including FREE video lessons to help you implement the key learnings from the book.

To access these FREE bonuses, simply visit...

www.PianoAndKeyboardMadeEasy.com

Acknowledgements

It takes a lot of input from a lot of people to shape and mould a person. As the saying goes, "It takes a village to raise a child." Many people have helped shape who I am, the way I think, act and engage with the world. I have to thank my mother Mary, for raising me to be an independent thinker and encouraging me to find my own path through this amazing, crazy world. She has always been a source of strength and inspiration to myself and many others. I have never heard her speak a bad word about anyone, only emanating love and encouragement to all. At the age of 99 she continues to inspire and lead. I am so looking forward to your hundredth, mum.

To my wife Natascha, who ensures I stay in my happy place. Who provides me mental, physical and spiritual nourishment and keeps me on track and engaged in life in a balanced way. Thank you my darling for your love and encouragement. I know at times I am a pain in the A minor but you stay ever calm and strong in my stormy waters.

No one can innovate and progress through life and their chosen field without good teachers, mentors or masters to guide them. I am extremely lucky that I found Duncan Lorien and allowed him to lead me through the deep, dark tunnels of music theory, emerging quickly and easily into the light of a new musical paradigm. From difficult and complex – to simple and easy. We journeyed down the rabbit hole and I found enlightenment. Even though I haven't gone all the way with what you taught me, I took what I needed and it is more than enough.

I never thought I would become an author. It has been a wonderful journey and not nearly as difficult as I thought. Again having a mentor to guide me through the perils of publishing and encouraging me to continue on and see the journey through has been invaluable. So Darren Stephens and the team at Global Publishing deserve a lot of kudos. Without them this (and many other books) would remain just another "gunna". As in, one day I am "gunna" write a book. Thank you all so much for your belief, encouragement and kicks in the backside.

Contents

"Music produces a kind of pleasure that human nature cannot do without..."
Confucius

Foreword

It is always a great pleasure to observe the exponential expansion that graduates achieve after a seminar, even more so when a graduate takes on the responsibility to help others learn to speak the language of music. Over the past 30 years I have shared what I have researched and discovered about music on six continents with nearly 40,000 graduates in my Understanding of Music Seminars™ (www.understandingofmusic.com). If more penguins wanted to learn music I would probably add Antarctica and fly around the world each year to seven continents! Many graduates of those seminars are now playing, writing and recording professionally in multiple styles of music and others have gone on to become licensed teachers of The Lorien Method™.

However, Chris is a graduate who decided to write this book so he could share his passion and inspire you to start your own journey into the world of music. Chris chose to focus on the keyboard in this book as it is truly the most accessible instrument on which to start learning music. However, much of what he writes can be applied to any musical instrument including the voice. He includes many simplicities about the subject of music that I teach in my seminars but also introduces many unique ideas and approaches. He presents everything with an eye to practical application and instils huge positivity throughout each chapter.

This is not a book geared towards an academic study of the theory of music but a "let's get started now and have some fun with music" approach! It is an excellent book for anyone who wants to begin their own musical adventure and I am sure it will contain many "aha moments" for you along the way as you begin to realise that music truly is a language that anyone can learn quickly and easily.

Where will your journey into the world of music lead you?

Duncan R. Lorien

Founder, The Understanding of Music Seminars™

Introduction

I have made a big claim on the cover of this book that *you* (YES YOU!) can sound good on the piano *instantly.*

I stand by this claim as it is the very thing that got me into the piano (at the age of 40) and kept me interested as I was exploring, learning and practicing the incredible world of music. *I was able to sound good even before I knew anything about music.* That kept me going.

Many people will scoff at this claim and tell you that the only way to learn is to get a good teacher and learn how to do it 'properly'.

Obviously the system has produced some brilliant musicians. So if you wish to learn to *read* music and you are willing to spend many, many years and untold amounts of money, and you are good at enduring the frustrations of sorting through the complexities and conundrums in a system that is thousands of years old and unchanged or updated in all that time, then go and do that. This book is not for you.

The people telling you there is only *one* way to learn are generally products of that broken system. We are always discovering new ways to do things (just ask Kodak or Nokia) the establishment clings stubbornly until overwhelmed by numbers. Revolution is normally a slow process.

I will go into why the system is broken in more detail in the book and how it got that way. All you need to know here is that there are many

ways to learn something and sometimes *the way we've always done it* is neither the best way nor the quickest and most efficient.

I will agree with the sceptics that nothing beats sitting with your instrument and putting in the time practising. Music is an area deserving of a lifetime of study and application. As with many things it is only in the application and practice that one gains insights and eventually… mastery. In fact it has been said that mastery is only reached after spending 10,000 hours practising one's chosen craft. Any true master would tell you that mastery is an illusion. There is *always* a next step, a new insight, something else to learn.

So let me deal with this claim of sounding good *instantly* right now so that all the sceptics may be somewhat appeased and if you are wondering if this book *is* for you, you may be convinced I am not full of BS.

Firstly I am not claiming you will be able to play a Beethoven concerto straight up or even belt out a tune from Elvis or the Beatles but you will be able to sit at the piano and play a pleasing tune and sound good – instantly. And in a very short time, as you study the contents of this book, you will gain an understanding of music that normally takes years and years of study, practice and application.

Now – back to sounding good *instantly*. How is this done? You have probably already done it. You can sound good even before you know anything about the keyboard. If you doubt this claim then try this…

Sit at the keyboard and play *only* white notes. *Play them very slowly!*

If you can, play the same notes with both hands.

Look at the keyboard. There are a lot of white keys. Among the white keys you will see the black keys. The black keys are in a pattern. You will see 2 black keys, then 3 black keys, then 2 black keys. Ensure you are playing the white keys on, or around, one of those groups ***with both hands.*** *So your left hand is playing white notes near a group of 3 and your right hand is playing*

I guarantee you will sound good.

So you can sound good immediately without knowing a whole lot about the piano keyboard or music.

But we don't stop there.

Continuing into the book we are going to learn to easily name the notes.

We will learn about scales and how simple and easy they are.

We will learn how chords are constructed and how they have a simple easy pattern that can be learned in no time at all.

And that is just for starters

All the other stuff like – Every Good Boy Deserving Fruit, staves, minims, double crochets and such… forget about it. Unless you have a yearning to play classical tunes by Mozart or something, pah! You don't need to know it.

Music is nothing but patterns. Simple number patterns like the ones we learned in primary (elementary) school. *Patterns that traditional music won't teach you.* You have to have learned for many years before you see them. (And then, for some reason, you don't pass on that knowledge to your students but put them through the same tough grind that you had to endure. Why? Well that's the way it's always been done. ☺)

I will teach you the most common patterns you need (as shown to me by Duncan Lorien) and show you how you can learn these patterns quickly and easily (instantly); unlike the ponderous and slow method that traditional music teaches.

Now as you very quickly learn which notes sound good when played together and which patterns sound good you will *never* sound awful.

We will apply the same logic to chords. (Chords are 3 or more notes played together to produce a harmonious sound.) All chords also follow rules and adhere to a particular pattern. Every type of chord has a pattern that each one uses. These patterns are simple and easy to learn and use. You can learn the most common ones very quickly (instantly?). You will not get stuck in any particular genre but will have the freedom to explore any musical style you wish.

I will show you the best way to practice for fast results and everything in the book will be explained further using videos which will be available on the website.

So you will have the building blocks of music and an understanding of the way music is constructed and that is great, but we will take it further and I will show you how most popular songs have been constructed using 3 or 4 chords. Not only does this make it easy to start playing your favourite songs but it also means you can start writing your own songs very quickly. I will show you how to use chord charts to get you playing and singing your favourite tunes. There are popular music songbooks that have been created with every song written in 'C'.

This means you can learn between 3 and 6 chords and play all the popular songs in these books. By the way, they do this because in traditional teaching it might take you two years to get to this stage (I kid you not, two years to learn a handful of chords), and people have had enough by then and want some results. In these pages you will quickly learn the popular chords and be able to play most popular songs from the last 100 years. Or if you own a modern keyboard you could learn those 3 to 6 chords and use the transpose button to play them in any key. I aim to give you greater choices than the hard slog of getting a teacher and learning the traditional way.

I have also written the book so that each section will stand alone. It is a book you can jump around in. It is not just a textbook. There is quite a bit of my story in here as well as the music instruction. I feel this is necessary to give the book context and hopefully it will inspire some of you to get into music for yourselves especially if you are older and thinking it is too late. I want you to know that it is not about talent but is more about persistence and knowledge. You *can* do it!

If you have been playing for a while and wish to understand how to find a chord, then jump to that section. If you want to *get* what scales are all about then dive right into that chapter.

My wish is for you to use the book and the videos you will find on the website to gain a greater understanding of music and how it is constructed and put together. For me, knowing this made all the difference to my musical journey. This knowledge cut years off the process and allowed me to enjoy creating and exploring music, rather than slogging away doing what I was told with little understanding of why I was doing it.

Key Learnings

- You can sound good instantly (as long as you play the right notes)
- You can learn music quickly and easily
- You will understand the building blocks of music and play as you please

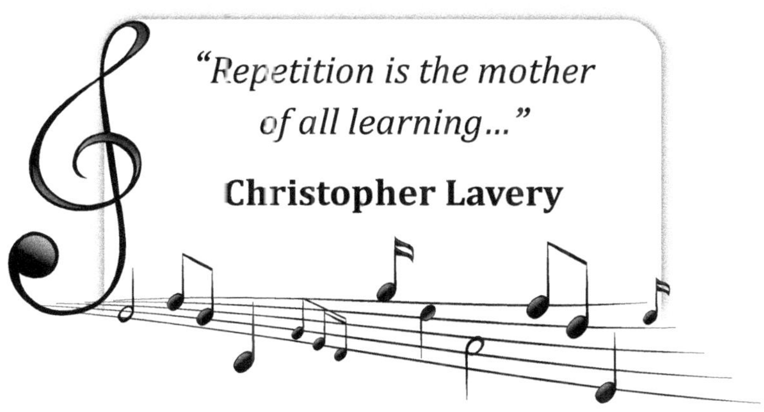
"Repetition is the mother
of all learning..."
Christopher Lavery

This book is for you if...

You have spent some time in traditional lessons and gave it away in frustration. I've met you. There are lots and lots of you. Lessons, sometimes for years and then you stopped making music because you came to the point in your journey where it became too difficult or too confusing and the system made it impossible for you to continue. So you stopped and resigned yourself to being *not good enough* or *too dumb to get it*.

So many 'failed' musicians on the musical scrapheap. What a sad state of affairs.

Guess what? IT IS NOT YOUR FAULT!!

For most of us music is too complex, too difficult and too hard to understand.

Or perhaps you are an adult who never had the opportunity or time to learn music and now it is something you regret. You'd love to learn but you know doing it the traditional way just takes too long and you don't have that much time.

I know when my 'how to' books started talking about minims and crotchets I phased out, my eyes crossed and after struggling and persevering, probably for too long, I was no longer interested. That's why I've written this book. I am not going to try and teach you music theory. I can't. I don't know it well enough and I am not a product of that system.

I am not going to teach you this…

This book will teach you how to play music without reading music.

You **do not need** to learn or understand all the *traditional music complexities.*

Many famous contemporary musicians cannot read music yet they write and perform their songs to adoring audiences the world over. Unless you aspire to be a concert pianist you too do not need to be able to read music to become a successful and accomplished musician.

All Western music is based on the piano keyboard. Understand the piano keyboard and you understand Western music. I most often play an electronic keyboard (as having a piano has always presented a space problem) so there is a section devoted to using the electronic keyboard as it is such an amazing instrument but everything you

will learn here applies to the piano and by extension to all of the instruments you may find in an orchestra.

I'll say it again… All Western music and Western instruments are based on the piano keyboard.

My goal is to make it simple and easy for you to understand because I believe we should all be able to play an instrument and have the joy of music in our lives. Unfortunately for many it is an elitist activity and there are those who wish to keep music's 'secrets' locked up forever.

It's also written for all of the parents who buy their children a keyboard at Christmas or on a birthday hoping their child will take to it somehow like the progenies we hear of and just 'get it' and become a great musician. Guess what mum and dad? They won't!

How many countless thousands of unused keyboards are there? Finally put up for sale on eBay, we pull them out of dark and dusty corners where we tucked them to hide our secret shame; our inability to understand or crack the code to helping our child to be a musician. The child plays with the keyboard for a little while and discovers it can make some cool sounds; they might even take some lessons; but they don't understand how music is constructed so soon stop playing altogether. Another 'failed' musician.

You can learn through this book, how to support your musical child to become a musician.

This book is also for anybody who wants to learn or expand their musical knowledge with the least effort possible. If you've been learning an instrument for a while, whether self-taught or taking lessons, this book will take you further along the journey and give you an understanding that will help you enjoy making and playing music. My wish is that no one can make you feel stupid again.

One of the problems with learning music from a music teacher is that usually that teacher is part of the system. They have gone through the system, they have learned the system from the system and by the system, and they are restricted by the system.

This book comes from outside of the system and so approaches the learning of music from a different angle. I am not going to teach you about crotchets and minims, I'll leave that to the other system. What you will learn, is how music is constructed and how in a very short time you can be playing an instrument and creating your own music.

Musicians who have played for a long time may well know these things but in my experience they keep their cards close to their chests

unwilling to share too much of what they know. Maybe they don't want others knowing their secrets, maybe they think you should go and endure the pain of learning for years and years like they did? I can only speculate on these things but I do know this, music has been a protected and closed shop for a very, very, long time. And it is time for that to stop.

Even great musicians are stifled and held in check by the system. A few years back, I met a lovely woman who was a concert pianist travelling constantly between major cities and performing in all the magnificent concert halls of the world. What an amazing life! I was full of admiration and respect for her obvious skill level and accomplishments. But I was puzzled when one day she sidled up to me at a function and whispered, "Can you show me how to play the blues?"

Whaaat?! How could it be that someone who has studied music all her life, someone who travels the world playing great concertos to admiring audiences did not know how to play the blues?

a. The blues are very simple to play as you'll find out later in this book and

b. How is it possible to study music for so long and not know how to play any damn style you like?

I was dumbstruck! Later I found out that those who take that path and go through the 'great' music conservatories only learn classical music and are told things like, "All the great music has already been written" and, "Who do you think you are that you could possibly write anything of any significance?" I cannot believe that the only purpose of spending all those years in study is so that you can recreate the masterpieces of some long dead maestro. That all your enjoyment of music is in such a narrow frame!

As mentioned above there are many famous (contemporary) musicians who have been hugely successful who never learned to read music.

They include the following…

Robert Johnson – Growing up on the cotton fields with his mother, young Robert never had any formal music lessons. Robert is considered the master of the Mississippi Delta Blues style and is a legend in the blues fraternity.

Elvis Presley – The King is another who was never formally trained and never knew music theory. He also never had voice training but was able to use what he had to entertain, soothe and excite millions around the world.

The Beatles – John Lennon, Paul McCartney, George Harrison and Ringo Starr – The Fab Four did not know how to read and write music. That may be hard to believe but it is the truth. In an interview with Playboy magazine in 1980 John Lennon was quoted as saying, *"None of us could read music, none of us can write it…"*

Jimi Hendrix – Was an American guitarist, singer and songwriter who amazed people with his innovative style. He redefined guitar playing

for a generation and is still very influential today. Yet *he had no formal training and was not able to read or write music.*

Eric Clapton – Another international successful musician who is open and honest about not being able to read or write music. In his autobiography he shares about his anxiety at a recording session with Aretha Franklin admitting he was nervous as everyone else was playing from sheet music on stands.

Stevie Ray Vaughan – The great blues guitarist and singer also could not read music.

Eddie Van Halen – Never learned to read music. He learned by watching and listening to others.

Tommy Emmanuel – Known the world over as a virtuoso guitarist. Never had a formal lesson and learned to play from his mother from a young age.

Slash Hudson – Famous for his lead guitar work with Guns n Roses, Slash never learned to read music.

As you can see there are some big names on the list but it doesn't end there.

Below are some more famous names to add to it if you need more convincing that you don't need years of formal training to successfully learn how to play music.

Jimmy Page from Led Zeppelin; Danny Elfman, creator of many movie soundtracks; famous jazz musicians The Rosenberg Trio; rapper Kanye West; ol' blue eyes Frank Sinatra; Danny Kaye and his wife Sylvia Fine; Barbara Streisand; Paul Simon and Bing Crosby… All music illiterates.

It is obvious from the list above that being able to read and write music is not necessary to be able to produce great music. They obviously knew something that the rest of us don't because their shortcomings didn't stop them. And they shouldn't stop you either.

Key Learnings

- Music *is* complex and difficult to master. The system deliberately keeps it that way
- Most music teachers are part of the system and thus cannot show you the simplicity
- Just because you were "stopped" in the past doesn't mean you are stopped forever
- Learning an instrument CAN be easy
- It is never too late to learn
- Many famous musicians never had formal music training

"Music gives a soul to the universe.
Wings to the mind, flight to the
imagination and life to everything..."
Plato

How I got into playing music

Look out here comes the biographical bit. I was not a child prodigy. I have not been learning and playing since I was a child. My musical journey didn't begin until I was 36 years old. I didn't play in the school band (there wasn't one) or any band until I was 56 years old. My story goes thus…

In my late 20s I had an awakening. Like a lot of awakenings it was born from pain. My marriage had broken down; I was feeling bitter and resentful and wondering what on earth life was all about. I felt like I had done all the things I 'should' have done and yet here I was a failure and a miserable one at that. (Later I learned that if you live your life from 'shoulds' – you'll likely 'should all over yourself' but that is another story). Up until then my life had followed what I thought was a 'normal' course. I had worked hard, met girl, bought house, had children and a dog and was living what outwardly looked to be a happy and successful life. There was the nagging feeling in the back of the mind that there is more to life that I was somehow incomplete or missing something. The drugs and alcohol should have been a warning. Nevertheless my comfortable little world fell apart despite attempts to 'fix' things by selling the house, buying a caravan and travelling around Australia. That resulted in us living in outback Western Australia and me working on a prawn trawler. The last real job I ever had. The reality shows you have seen on life on a fishing boat give you some idea of what it is like but… Let's just say I knew whatever I did after that was going to be easy.

I have found in life that when faced with a painful and perhaps unprecedented situation people do one of two things. They either fall back on old patterns and repeat the same behaviours (we all know someone who has left one destructive relationship or job only to go and get into another, equally or more destructive) or they take radical action and change their lives. Again, we all know someone who has left a long-term relationship, suddenly loses heaps of weight, takes up some amazing hobby (like music), or travels the world meets a new exotic partner and goes to live in Bangladesh or something. It happens right? Well I decided I was going to be a performing artist.

From fisherman to performing artist is quite a trip. One day I was delirious on the deck of a heaving trawler at 4 am and a short while later I am performing in plays, juggling and eating fire. How did I get there? Well, once I was through the pain of the separation and looking at, "What now with my life?" I determined to return to school and study. I had never enjoyed school and had not done well but I knew it wasn't a result of not being smart or intelligent enough, for the most part I found it boring and frustrating. My final year of high school resulted in two Es, an F and a G. Is that even possible or am I getting confused with musical notes? Anyway it was bad and I felt that I would like to remedy that situation. I needed to feel better about myself and I thought I *should* (there's that word again) do something about it. When trying to decide what I wanted to study I found my old school reports and realised there was only two subjects I enjoyed at school and they were drama and sport. Then when I looked further into teacher's comments I saw that the career advice that I desperately needed as a young man was there all along. There it was right before my eyes, "*Chris is the class clown*" and this… "*When he gets over his need for an audience…*" Seriously? So performing arts it was.

I think I am lucky in that I had come to the realisation that in order to be satisfied with life I needed to pursue something that I was passionate about. That the 40/40 plan (i.e. working 40 hours per week for 40 years) did not work for me and I would never be 'happy' if I did that. Being 29 when I started this course of study I was in a bit of a hurry so I chose a two year full-time TAFE (Technical & Further Education) course in theatre and performing arts that gave me wide ranging choice of subjects and circus was the one that grabbed me.

OMG I can juggle! After two years I graduated with skills in juggling and stilts, radio and theatre. But… still no music.

It wasn't until I was 36 and I attended an outdoor hippy-type festival and it seemed that everyone at the festival (and certainly most everyone that I was camping with) played a musical instrument. I'll say one thing for hippies and that is they are not constrained by the societal norms that stop the rest of us. Work as most of us know it is an alien concept and they spend a lot of time on music, art, exploring consciousness and protesting to save the planet. Not necessarily in that order and not necessarily a bad thing either. I have always thought society needs its extremists, those to the far right or left of centre because life would be rather beige without them. So at the festival, which was held on the banks of Australia's biggest river, I had a great time joining in with my (new) musical friends, singing and tapping along and I enjoyed it immensely.

Afterwards I wondered why it was that I never learned to play a musical instrument. I had such a good time that I left the festival determined to learn an instrument. Not long afterwards I was passing a local pawn shop and I noticed a clarinet in the window. I liked the look of it; all that engineering was somehow very appealing and I had always liked it as an instrument thanks to people like Benny Goodman and Acker Bilk. So for the princely sum of $35 I was off on my musical journey. There was one more purchase needed before I could become a maestro and that was a *How to Play Clarinet* book purchased from the local music store. So armed with my book and my new knowledge of how to put the thing together, I sat down and was soon producing a series of squeaks and squawks. I persisted. Persistence will get you a long way in this music caper as it will in life and lo and behold before too long I could actually make that clarinet sound fairly reasonable. After a short time I was able to play some real tunes. But here is the thing. The only thing I took from the *How to* book was how to put it together, how to fit the reed and how to find and name the notes. The rest of it was confusing and tedious. And do I really want to know how to play a few popular nursery rhymes and Christmas carols? Not for me and I'm guessing not for a lot of others either. So I learned to play by ear. **See notes on playing by ear at the end of this chapter**

I shall never forget the day one of my older brothers, whilst trying to put me down and keep me in my place, taunted me and said, "Go on then, play some Acker Bilk"... And I could! He never bagged me again after that. (Here I was 36 and my older brother was still trying to put me down and keep me in my place of 'little brother'. Really? No wonder we get stopped. Anyway thanks for the encouragement bro, it was wonderful being able to put you in your place.) I kept practising and, as is inevitable when one practises, I improved and I kept improving in measure with the amount of practice I did. I enjoyed that clarinet so much and I was using it in my act as a clown and stilt performer. I was proud of myself for teaching myself to play and wanted more. So I bought a saxophone. Again it was purchased from a pawn shop for little money and I had to also buy a how to play the saxophone book so I could learn how it went together, how to blow into it, the weird fingering of notes are and their names.

The engineering that goes into these instruments is fantastic. That's why I was attracted to them in the first place, that and the fact that I love the sound, especially the saxophone, seems that everybody loves the saxophone, so I decided to concentrate on that. I also found it easier to play. Having said that, I still own a clarinet and do occasionally play it. So the saxophone became a part of my act and at the time I was doing a lot of stilt-walking work around my hometown of Melbourne and I was able to go out on my stilts and confidently play saxophone. (Confident that if I had a fall I would probably put the sax through the back of my throat.) Life is pretty dull without some risk eh?

My success at playing these instruments received a lot of interesting reactions. Of course many people congratulated me on the achievement but many others said things like, “Oh you must have had the talent all along.” NO!

Let me make this clear right here. I am not an inherently ‘talented’ person. I am however a persistent and stubborn one who is not afraid of hard work or looking foolish.

I practiced really hard and long. I was lucky in that a) I had the time due to not being on the 40/40 plan I had stopped that when I hit my late 20s and came to my senses) and b) I had an empty house to practise in. This is important because…

No one wants to listen to you practise when you are not very good at it.

The truth is I didn’t have a clue how to play music. The opportunity never presented itself as I was growing up and so I just never learned. When I discovered that I could actually make a reasonable sound come out of these instruments and that I could play some real tunes I was so thrilled that I practised even harder.

At the age of 40 I took up the piano keyboard and I am extremely lucky that I found Duncan Lorien and The Understanding of Music Seminar™ www.understandingofmusic.com

Duncan travels the world teaching music, the promise of his seminar is the equivalent of a music degree in a weekend. I know this sounds unbelievable and my musician friends scoffed, laughed and said it couldn't be done but I was willing to trust that he knew a heck of a lot more than I did and perhaps he could pass a bit of that knowledge along. It greatly appealed to me as at this stage my musical knowledge was limited to a couple of how to books and my own efforts at playing (by ear) the clarinet and saxophone.

After attending Duncan's seminar my knowledge of music was hugely expanded and I was excited and thrilled at the possibilities. I now understood so much more about music. I understood its structure and I understood how it was put together and that greatly accelerated my journey. Suddenly it all made sense. Prior to doing Duncan's seminar I was playing the saxophone and just picking out tunes by ear. Now I had structure and purpose. I was learning things on the keyboard and transferring them to the sax. Eventually the sax took a back seat and the keyboard took over completely.

I would recommend to anyone of any musical ability, if you get the chance to attend one of Duncan's seminars then you do whatever it takes to be there. The man is a walking encyclopaedia of the history of music and the reasons why it is complex and difficult and he is able to simplify the difficult into easy to understand bites. His claim of the equivalent of a music degree in a weekend is not an idle one.

The biggest challenge I had was getting 40-year-old fingers to do what I wanted them to do and whilst this was frustrating at times I was encouraged by my progress to persist. As an aside here I would comment to parents who may be reading this book that if you can get

your children interested in skills such as playing a musical instrument when they are young then it comes to them a lot easier than it does later in life. What Duncan's seminar did was open up a whole new world of music and for many, many years I was content to simply explore that world of music. I would spend hours learning and playing different scales and chords. I played all the popular ones and also the more obscure and discordant ones. Countless hours were spent discovering new patterns and different ways of playing them. I marvelled that I could play the blues (in any key) and that I could sit at any piano and create a good sound.

Eventually I decided to have a go at learning some songs and I found a couple of websites www.chordie.com and www.ultimate-guitar.com where I was able to find and print out chord charts to popular songs that I was familiar with and I enjoyed. (There are many other websites but these are two that I used.) You may be familiar with a chord chart. It is the lyrics to a song with the chords written above the words. Play the chords sing the words under the chord. Pretty simple. (Make note… not all of the songs one finds on the internet are accurate. That messed me up at times.) I found that by playing them slowly I could play *and* sing the songs and they sounded okay, if a little slower than normal. As I practised more I was able to bring them up to speed and add different inflections both in the music and with the vocals. I had spent years learning the chords so they came together fairly easily and at some point I was able play them without needing to look at the keyboard any more. This was a big breakthrough. Wow! I could play without looking.

Now, after banging away on the keyboard for almost 20 years I wish to share what I have learned with the world. How I went from zero musical knowledge at the age of 40, to playing (and singing) at a good standard. I started playing in a band at the age of 56 and that was pretty exciting. Over the years I have done a number of solo gigs but playing in the band and being the lead singer for the band, well that is very exciting.

When it comes to learning the keyboard, or any other instrument, there are a few things one probably must do. You will need to learn the names of the notes and where they are. You will also need to learn chords *and how to find them*. For most musicians when they come across a chord they don't know they run for the chord book or website and look it up. This is part of the problem of learning music the traditional way, because you don't understand how things are constructed you must learn each chord and scale by what notes are contained within them. You've got to learn which notes go in which scale and you've got to learn which notes go in which chord. In this book you will learn the patterns that underlie the major and minor scales and chords so that you don't particularly need to know which notes they contain. You just need to know the pattern. There is an enormous musical palette and yet most musicians only use a couple of colours; the main ones being major, minor and blues.

Guitarists like to use a scale called the pentatonic and there is one or two others used occasionally but the actual array of scales and chords that are available is much, much larger than what is commonly known or used. It is only jazz musicians that venture into the dark unknown side of the musical vocabulary.

What I learned from Duncan is that, mostly, I only need to be able to count in ones, twos and threes and the occasional four or five to be able to play any music that has been developed over the past two thousand years. That's it. It is incredibly simple. I was always good at my times tables when I was a child at school. I was also good at counting and number patterns. I even learned to count backwards from ten let alone count up to ten. Yes that is how simple music is. If you can count up to five then you too can learn music.

Key Learnings

- People only change is there is great pain or great gain on offer
- It is never too late to start something. As Nike says… Just do it…
- Find a mentor or system that you can follow
- Ignore the haters and naysayers

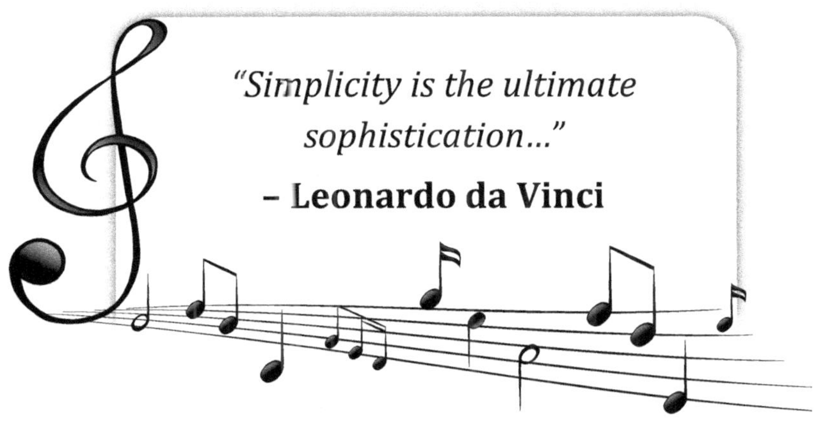
"Simplicity is the ultimate sophistication..."
– Leonardo da Vinci

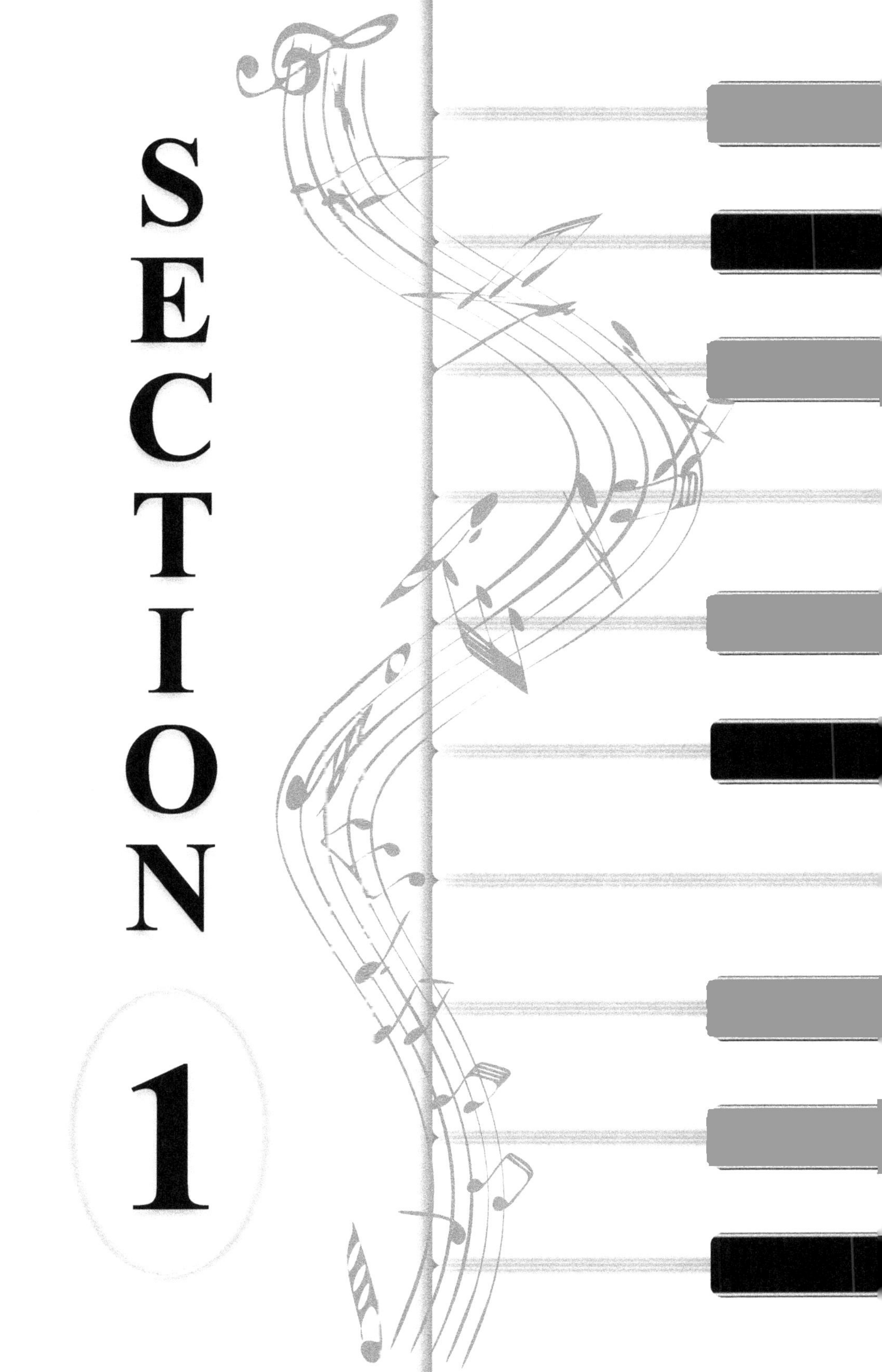
SECTION
1

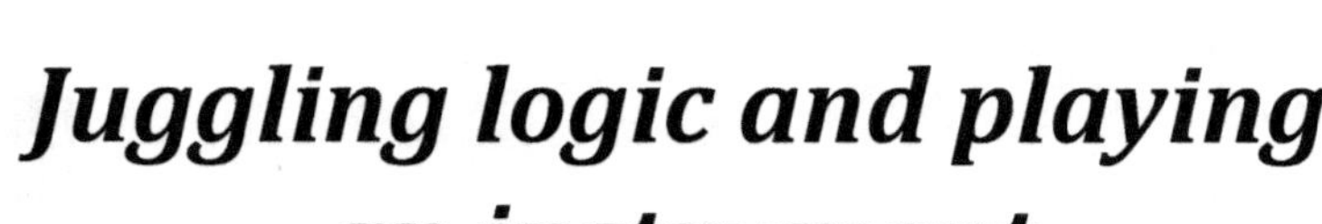

Juggling logic and playing an instrument

Valuable lessons I learned from juggling.

- *The lesson of simplifying things and taking one step at a time.*
- *The lesson of persistence.* This one lesson overcomes most things.
- *The lesson of patience.* Rome wasn't built in a day. It takes time.
- *The lesson of building on what has been previously learned.*
- *The lesson of daily practice.*
- *The lesson (and value) of sleeping on things.*

I applied juggling logic to learning music.

Learn to simplify and de-complicate things by breaking them down into easy bite size pieces.

Most people can't just pick up three balls and juggle them. You have to start with one ball and learn how to juggle that. Then a second ball is added, then three, four and more. To juggle clubs, knives or fire you must begin again and learn how to do those. To learn a new trick is a similar process of breaking the trick down in to its parts, learning those parts and then put it together piece by piece. Music is the same. Look for the simplicity, break it into easy pieces and then put it together. Then build upon what you've learned, one step at a time.

Repetition is one of the mothers of learning. If you think about when you started driving (assuming you are old enough to have done that) you had to think about all the things you had to do. Being in the right gear, using the indicator watching out for traffic, using your mirrors, looking at the traffic lights etc., etc. But once you've been driving for some time all of that becomes automatic. Now you can drive while drinking a coffee, checking your messages and having a conversation with your passengers. Playing music is no different. It truly is like riding a bike. Once you have put in the initial time it begins to become very easy, your fingers know where to go and you don't have to think about it and concentrate so much. This is why it is important to get into a daily practice routine.

It is easy to give up and think, "I cannot do this." This is where persistence comes in. It is said that Edison failed in his quest to invent the light bulb one thousand times. Lucky for us he persisted. Michael Jordan claims to have missed over 9000 shots during his career but didn't he nail some important ones? You have to ***be kind to yourself***. You are not dumb or stupid. You just have to stick at it and the results will come.

Persistence, persistence, persistence.

Sometimes it seems as if nothing is improving, nothing is changing. You work hard at something, you think good thoughts, you give it your all, and… Nothing happens. But as I said, Rome wasn't built in a day. The blueprints had to be drawn up, the groundwork had to be done, the underground sewers had to go in and the foundations had to be laid.

For a long time it looked like nothing was happening. It looked like there was a lot of work going in for little or no results when in fact a lot was happening. The foundations were being laid for the great result that was to follow.

Learning a new skill can be like that. Lots of work, for seemingly no result. And then one day you realise you have reached a new level. You can do something you haven't been able to do before and it suddenly seems easy. The thing is, you never know how close or far you are from reaching that level. It may be just another day; another hour and you are there. Many people set a goal, put in hours, days or even years of work and when they are on the cusp of achieving that goal they give up in frustration.

Be patient

There is a popular saying which is attributed to Einstein that goes, *"Insanity is doing the same thing over and over and expecting a different result..."* Well in music you most likely will do the same thing over and over and get a great result. Repetition is one of the keys to learning and you can do the same thing over and over and get a different result. By playing the same notes and chords on the keyboard over and over I was eventually able to find and play them without having to use my eyes. *Doing the same thing, achieving a different result*. In juggling and in music it is important to spend the time to get the basics right. That means hours and hours of repetition. Luckily it is enjoyable repetition. When the basics are strong then you are free to improvise and explore knowing you have a strong and competent default level.

Keep at it…

Practise daily

Without this nothing of significance can be achieved by the 'average' person. But don't be put off. I say you need at least five minutes of practise per day. It is not so much how long you can practise but how often. Find that time. Build the habit of daily practise and you will reap incredible rewards.

This goes against the accepted norm of putting your nose to the grindstone and 'working hard' for long hours. Yes go for it when you are in the flow. Most of us can only flow at peak for an hour or two so after that time stop and move on to the next thing. A change is as good as a holiday. I like to practise as least once a day but often I will get in two or three short practice sessions. This keeps it fresh and interesting so you don't get bogged down or frustrated. And… when you do get frustrated, that is the time to stop and sleep on it.

It is amazing how the brain will process things for you while you sleep. Many times I found while learning to do a particularly hard juggling trick I would become very frustrated after dozens of attempts at that trick so would stop and…

Sleep on it

Often the next day, the trick came quite easily. It's the same with music. Often when trying to get your head around how to play a difficult chord or an inversion, stepping away from the keyboard is the best thing to do. When you come back to it you can play it with far less difficulty.

Key Learnings

- It's never too late to learn an instrument (or anything else)
- Consistent practise reaps considerable rewards
- Keep it simple and build up to the difficult
- If it gets frustrating stop and sleep on it
- Practise the stuff that you find difficult
- Once you've got it, it's yours forever
- Do not listen to others. Their experience does not need to be yours
- There is always a quicker, easier way… keep looking

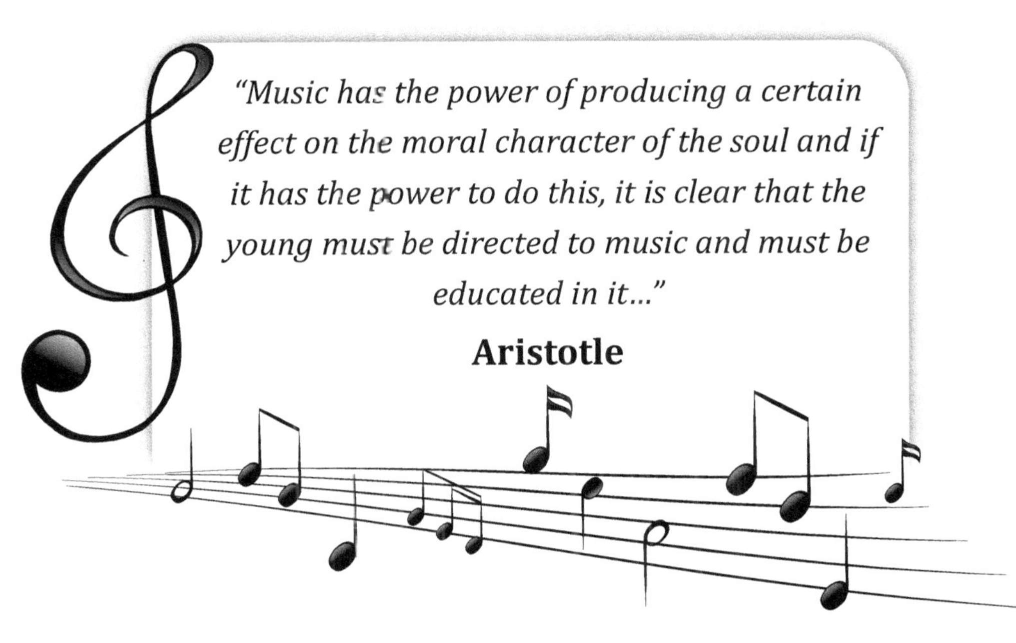
"Music has the power of producing a certain effect on the moral character of the soul and if it has the power to do this, it is clear that the young must be directed to music and must be educated in it..."
Aristotle

Some notes on playing by ear

People seem to think that if you can play by ear then you must be some sort of genius. The truth is…

Most people have a very good ear for music

Think about how much music you listen to in your lifetime. I came from a family where there was always music playing, whether that was on the radio, the record player, on the TV or in the car. I probably listened to a couple of hours of music per day. When I think about the world today it is even more prevalent. Everywhere you go there is music playing. All the shops play music, there is music in the elevators and public spaces. Video games, movies, music videos, computers, everything revolves around music and it seems everyone is getting about with earphones or buds listening to music.

I would estimate that by the time the average person has reached ten years old they have listened to over 70,000 hours of music. If that hasn't trained your ear then nothing will. I am certain that if I asked you to hum your favourite tune you could do so perfectly. But if I ask you to sing it?

We have all been bombarded with music since birth.

Isn't it amazing that so many people claim to be tone deaf? Such a laughable claim – in the face of the evidence. So I say that we all know what sounds good and what sounds bad, we have been trained since birth! What makes popular music popular? Simple. It sounds good to a lot of people. So we know what sounds good. We all have good ears that can recognise what sounds good and what doesn't, so all that is left to do is learn where those good sounds are on any particular instrument.

Truth is most of us have no idea if we can play by ear or not. Why not have a go? Lock yourself in a room and practise on the instrument. You will know if you sound good or not. No one else needs to know. No one else needs to hear you (and judge you).

What stops most of us from attempting anything is the armchair critics.

People will happily criticise you and tell you why you are no good and why you will never be any good. Often it is those closest to us. Yes, family and friends. Tragic!!

Hide away from the public glare. It is inevitable that you will improve. You will build familiarity with the instrument. You will learn what sounds good and what sounds not so good. It is what I did with the clarinet and the saxophone. Many years ago I learned to play harmonica sitting on the side of the road on a hitchhiking trip around Australia. Australia is a big country so I had a bit of time to play and there was no one there to judge me 'good' or 'bad' – except the crows. Years later (and I am talking 35 years later) I picked up the harmonica again when I joined a band and guess what? I could still

make it sound OK.

Read on and you will learn *scales*. Scales are a bunch of notes played in a particular pattern so that they *sound* good. If you don't play the pattern it will *sound* 'bad'. You will also learn chords and which ones sound good when played together in a particular pattern. And that they sound 'bad' if played out of pattern or randomly.

We all *know* music. So, rather than an inability that people have, I think it is a cultural thing. We have been trained through put-downs and criticisms to think that only special people have the ability to sing and the rest of us should just shut up and leave it to those especially blessed.

Unfortunately there are more critics in our society than there are participants. Ignore the critics, become a participant.

Key Learnings

- We have all been bombarded with music since birth
- We all have a good ear
- You may well be able to play by ear
- There are participants and there are critics
- Learn to ignore the critics

"Music has been around for millennia. Notes have been added, things have changed. But the teaching of music remains in the dark ages…"
Christopher Lavery

A bit of the history of music and why it is difficult

Music is as old as time itself. People have been playing music when they get together for as long as people have been around, whether that's banging on a log, clapping their hands, hitting two sticks together, singing, chanting, playing flutes and whistles; whatever. Back in ancient Greece they called it:

Mousa – any art connected to the muses such as music and lyrical poetry

and that playing multiple instruments was part of a Greek citizens normal education. It is believed that Pythagoras gave us the rules of sound and the concept of tone. The Greeks used very different patterns to what we use today and they believed that each pattern created a different effect on the listener making them feel reflective or passionate for example. Since that time we have had thousands of years to build up the layers of the musical onion.

The keyboard used to be an instrument that had fewer but much larger keys that were struck with the fists or even the weight of the whole body. At one stage the keyboard was used to play the church bells and this was done by striking large lever type keys. Gradually the keyboard became a standalone instrument and continued to develop. For many hundreds of years (during the Dark Ages) the Christian church *owned* music. There was *no* music other than church sanctioned music. There was *no* art at all, painting, literature, theatre, etc. that wasn't church sanctioned. That's why it is called the Dark Ages. So, music was only to be used for the worship of God and using it for any other purpose reduced its value for worshipping God. No one could play any sort of music that wasn't sanctioned by the church. That meant if you tried to be creative and do anything outside of the church's guidelines then you could be punished very severely (yes, even death). Church and state were inseparable at this time. (Things are slow to change.)

In Western music there are 12 musical notes thus giving us 12 major chords, 12 minor chords, etc. Why 12? Some speculate the Christian influence on Western music led the monks who developed it to choose 12 as there were 12 apostles. Couldn't be true though. Could it? Interesting to find that in other cultures there can be found a correlation between the number of notes in their music and the number of Gods or deities in their particular religion.

Latin was the approved language for explaining music and penalties were serious for singing the wrong prayer with the wrong music at the wrong time. So you had to learn music and all the complex rules from the monks. Not too many people were literate in those days and the monks had a monopoly on literacy, education and books. In order to learn music you first had to learn Latin and then you could learn music. The monks had a monopoly on teaching and Latin was an elite Roman language. Most citizens of the Roman Empire spoke a different language. So music was only available to those who could afford it and it was difficult, confusing and took years and years of expensive lessons. And as mentioned if you didn't get it right once you 'graduated' the penalties were serious. So what has changed?

You may notice there is still Latin terminology used in music. Italian became favoured during the Renaissance period as there was a lot of music coming out of the region and it was considered very fashionable, and there is a sprinkling of French and German terms as well. Except for a brief period during the 20th century in American jazz circles, Italian has stuck as the common language used for music. I guess no one has considered this a problem in the English speaking world. Another example of *that's just the way it is. We have always done it this way* mentality. Tradition dies hard. Change is vigorously resisted. You still have to learn some foreign language, it is still difficult and confusing and takes years and years of expensive lessons.

It gets worse. Over the centuries, music and the keyboard have developed and changed enormously. For example, there were no black keys on the keyboard. The black keys first appeared on the keyboard about 500 years ago. (The black keys are the sharps and flats.) Extra keys were also added to both ends of the keyboard to finally arrive at the 88 note keyboard we know today. No problem with that. Things change and evolve and of course we all embrace change and move on, right? Er… no.

The problem is that the teaching of the keyboard did not change to allow for the black notes (and the added notes), so we have situations where in order to know whether you're supposed to play a white key or a black key at any particular time, there is no sure method. You just have to 'know'. And that can take a long time and a lot of confusion before you get it. The systems I will teach you here make it very clear and easy whether you're playing a black key or a white key on any particular scale or chord. And you will know every time with no confusion.

Straight up, when learning piano keyboard, an example of confusion arises when we are told to find middle C. We look and find that middle C is not actually in the middle of the keyboard (remember those extra notes that were added). So why is that the first thing that we are asked to learn? *Because it used to be in the middle.* This is an example of the teaching not changing when conditions changed. Modern teachers will give you all sorts of reasons why this is taught but the truth is it used to be in the middle and there were no black keys. So the only way to orient yourself at the keyboard was to find middle C.

Think about it… There are no black keys, only white. How do you know which is which? Now, it is handy to know that below a certain point is considered the low or bass notes and above a certain point is considered the high notes and if you are reading music this is handy but this is not why you are taught "Find middle C." It is a relic left over from hundreds of years ago when you *needed* to find middle C because there were no black keys.

Another interesting example from history is this… Have a look at the symbol below. Do you know what it is?

Most people know that it's a treble clef and a treble clef is… well it's a treble clef. Yep it is. *But what is it?* I've even seen people with a treble clef tattooed on their body and when I've asked them if they know what it is they often say, yes it's one of those music things. Some even know it is a treble clef. But did you know that a treble clef is actually the letter 'g'? Why it is shaped like that is open to speculation but there may be a connection to a group of monks who used elaborated letters to begin chapters in their holy books. Regardless of why it takes this particular shape, all it is, is a letter G. And what is it for anyway? If you look at the lines on a piece of music and look at where the treble clef is positioned you'll see its whole purpose and its sole purpose is to mark the line of 'g' on the staves of written music. Its purpose is to tell the musician that, that line is a 'g'. Same thing applies to the bass clef. It looks like this.

What is it? It's an 'f'. It has the same purpose as the treble clef. It is marking a line.

There are many more examples throughout musical theory. Things that are taught without question because that is the way it is done and that is the way it has always been done. Mostly music teachers don't even know why they teach these things they just pass on the same things that they have been taught without questioning why they teach them.

So it seems to me that the teaching of music is still rooted in the dark ages. You have to learn Latin. You have to spend years paying for expensive lessons to try and untangle the craziness that the system has become. Thank goodness there are people who have broken away from the madness of this system. Throughout the 20th century we had jazz and rock n roll emerge and the rebels have passed on a legacy which makes it possible to break away from the system that is still firmly entrenched in the conservatories of the world.

It seems bizarre to me that there is a system in existence whose purpose is to teach just one style of music, that being classical music. The poor students who slave away for years emerge so trapped in the system they cannot see or play any other type of muwsic. It's unbelievable. So on that word of warning, let's get stuck into the piano keyboard and start learning the notes.

Key Learnings

- Music is an ancient art
- In ancient Greece music was a normal part of people's education
- Music has many secrets
- The establishment don't give up their secrets easily
- There are many layers to the musical onion

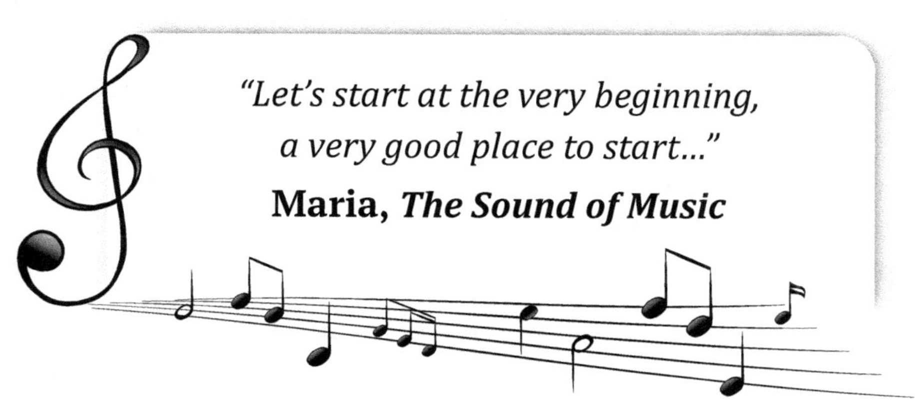
"Let's start at the very beginning,
a very good place to start..."
Maria, The Sound of Music

Learning the notes

White notes... easy peasy

It doesn't matter what instrument you are playing the first step is to learn the notes. This is good news as there are only 7 to learn. That's right ONLY 7 what are called natural notes and 5, what I am going to call, supplementary notes (the black notes also known as sharps and flats, we'll get onto them shortly). That's a total of only 12 notes. Only 12! There they are in the diagram below. If you can learn that much of the keyboard then you will know the whole keyboard. Does that make it a little easier?

7 white notes. 5 black notes. That's all folks!

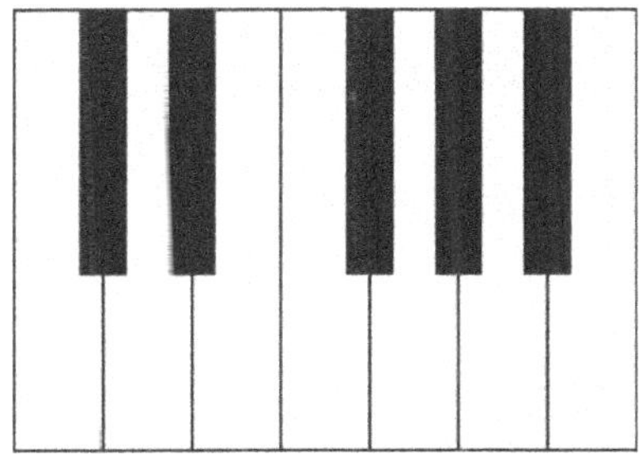

You had to learn twice that many letters when you learned to read and write words so this should be easy. If you can learn 26 letters of the alphabet and all the crazy laws of grammar (especially in English) then it should be fairly easy to learn 12 musical notes on a keyboard and a few rules of the language of music.

In The Understanding of Music Seminar™ Duncan teaches that the easiest note to find and learn on the keyboard is the 'D'; 'D' for Duncan. This makes a lot of sense and avoids confusion when compared to the traditional method of starting with the 'C'.

Have a look at the diagram below or if you have a piano or keyboard handy then look at that. Notice that there are black notes grouped in bunches of 2 and 3, 2 and 3, up and down the keyboard. Find any group of two black notes. In between those 2 black notes you will find a white note. That white note is 'D'.

The note in between the 2 black notes is "D"

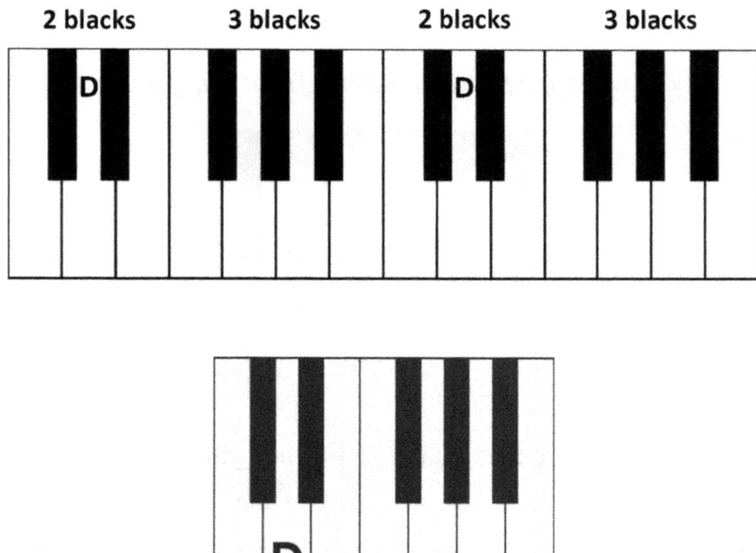

Play the D or put your finger on it on the diagram and say its name. It's a D. Now playing only the white notes and going *up* the keyboard, that is, to your right, the next white note up the keyboard is an E. Continuing on, it follows that the next note is F and the next note is G. With me so far I hope.

Now return to the D and go *down* the keyboard, that is, to your left, and playing only white notes the next note down is C, the one next to that is B and next to that is the A. There is your formula for easily locating and naming the notes. Find the D. There is no confusion about the D. Normally you would be taught to locate the C first but I find there is far less confusion when you locate the D than if you try to find the C as is recommended by music teachers everywhere. As you find and play these notes say the name, to yourself or out loud. Play a note five times, ten times saying the notes name each time. Repetition is the key. Do it again and again until you no longer have to.

That is the white notes covered A, B, C, D, E, F and G there are only 7 of them so it shouldn't take you long to find and identify those 7 notes. I know at first it is not easy but you must persist. Don't expect to have all this down pat in the first five minutes. Stick at it. Give yourself a month or six months then see how far you have come. All good things take a little time, so be patient and gentle on yourself… but do stick with it. It will happen.

Please avoid labelling or sticking tags on the keys, which only makes you reliant on the tags. Better to learn by repetition. You really don't need that sort of thing. There are only 7 notes and it really isn't very difficult if you practise the way I suggest. Practise every day, at least five minutes per day. You will very quickly be able to identify these 7 notes. Remember… there are there are only 7. You have more fingers than that.

Key Learnings

- There are only 12 notes in music and only 12 keys to learn on the piano keyboard
- There is a pattern of two and three black keys up and down the keyboard
- The D is in between the two black notes
- Find and name the D and you can easily find and name E, F, G and C, B, A.

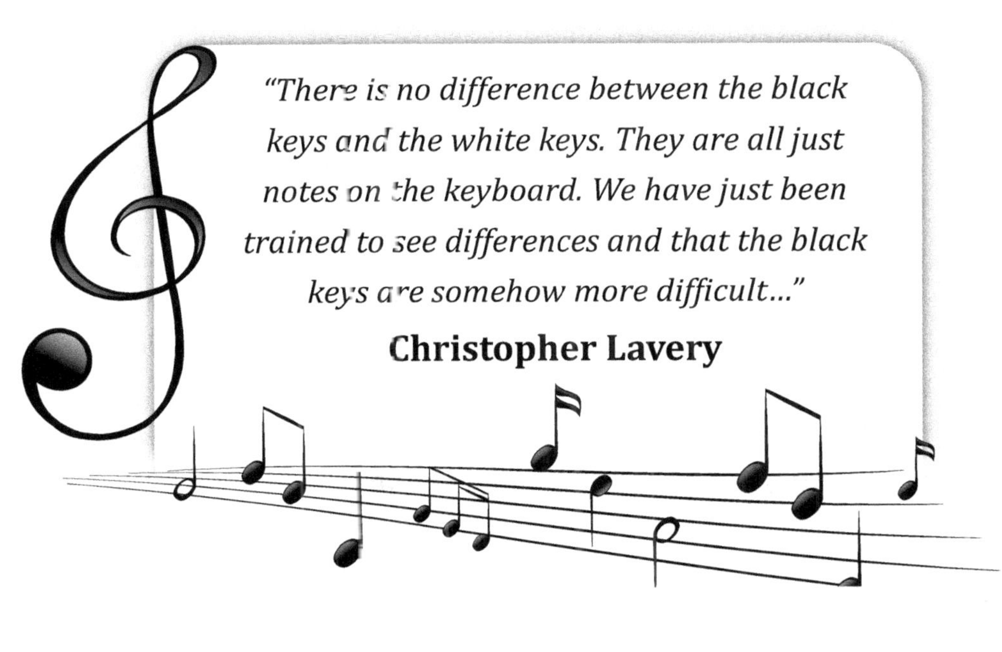
"There is no difference between the black keys and the white keys. They are all just notes on the keyboard. We have just been trained to see differences and that the black keys are somehow more difficult..."
Christopher Lavery

Oh no! Not the black keys!

Now let's demystify the black keys. The black keys are a fairly recent addition to the keyboard having been added about 500 years ago (and for a long time the white keys were black and the black keys were white) and they were added so that there were even spaces (frequencies) between each note on the keyboard. When they were added is not important but just know that they were added and obviously the idea was popular and we have gone with it ever since. This is called chromatic spacing and we will get to that soon. What it means is the space between each note is *exactly the same* so when you go up or down the keyboard you are moving the same distance in pitch each and every time. This allowed for a whole range of new scales, chords and melodies to be played on the keyboard and led to the creation of modern music. It also meant that every scale could now be played in any key. Prior to this, music was largely restricted to accompanying Gregorian chants (these were a form of monophonic sacred song of the Roman Catholic Church, likely named after Pope Gregory the Great. When Charlemagne became Holy Roman Emperor he made everyone in Europe use Gregorian chants) and hymns and fulfilling the needs of the church. So let's have a look at the black notes and name them.

The black notes are considered harder than the white notes, they have a certain mystique attached to them and most musicians are afraid of the black notes, especially those just starting out. I want you to start looking at the black notes as you do the white notes. They are just other notes on the keyboard and they are placed in the position they are in to make them easy to play, not hard. So how do we know how to name these black notes? That can be confusing. The process is in fact pretty easy as the black notes are supplementary notes of the white notes. They have the same name but with the addition of a sharp '#' or a flat '♭'. Let's first define what sharp and flat mean. In music to make something sharp is to make it sound a little higher. To make something flat is to make it sound a little lower. You may have heard someone tuning a guitar? You may have noticed when they do if they play a note and then tighten the string they make the note a little higher pitched or sharper. If they play a note and then loosen the string that makes that note a little lower sounding or flatter. And that is what the black notes do on the keyboard. They make the white note next to it a little lower (flat) or a little higher (sharp). A little sharper or a little flatter. Thus we have C (natural) and we have C sharp. We have B (natural) and we also have B flat. So now let's name those black notes. Look at the diagram below. As you can see, if we are going up the keyboard (that is, to the right) and the sounds are getting higher or sharper, the black note is called a sharp. If we are going down the keyboard (to the left) the sound is getting lower or flatter and the black note is called a flat.

"Ebony and ivory live together in perfect harmony side by side on my piano, keyboard, oh lord, why don't we...?"

Paul McCartney and Stevie Wonder

This means that all of the black notes actually have two names depending on whether you're going up the keyboard or going down the keyboard. As an example let's find the D once again. Remember, find a set of two black notes, and find the note in between the two black notes. That is D. To the left of the D you will find a black note and that black note is called D flat. To the right of the D there is another black note. That note is called D sharp. So as you move up and down the keyboard the black notes take on the name of the white note next to it, as either a sharp or a flat, depending on which way you are travelling, up or down the keyboard. Hopefully the diagram below explains it easily for you and of course you can go to the website and view the video on "Identifying the Black Notes".

Observant people will ask why there isn't a black note then between the B and the C and the E and the F? As I mentioned earlier the distance or space between each note is exactly the same. I guess they didn't need to add a black note in between these notes as it was already configured the way they wanted. But somewhere down the line you may come across an F flat or a B sharp and you may think what the heck? Just remember the rule above and you will see that an F flat is the E and a B sharp is the C. Messed up I know and I hope I haven't muddied the waters by mentioning it here. One more example of the things that stop people playing and enjoying music. Go and watch the video for clarification and know that at this stage of your

Key Learnings

- First find the D. It is any white note in between a set of 2 black notes
- Find and name the notes A through G
- Treat the black notes as you do the white notes, just another note.
- If you are going up the keyboard (to the right) the black notes are sharp #
- If you are going down the keyboard (to the left) the black notes are flat ♭

"One of the problems is we watch people performing at a very high level and we compare ourselves to them. Comparing yourself to another only leads to dissatisfaction and unhappiness with where you are at. Please don't do that!"
Christopher Lavery

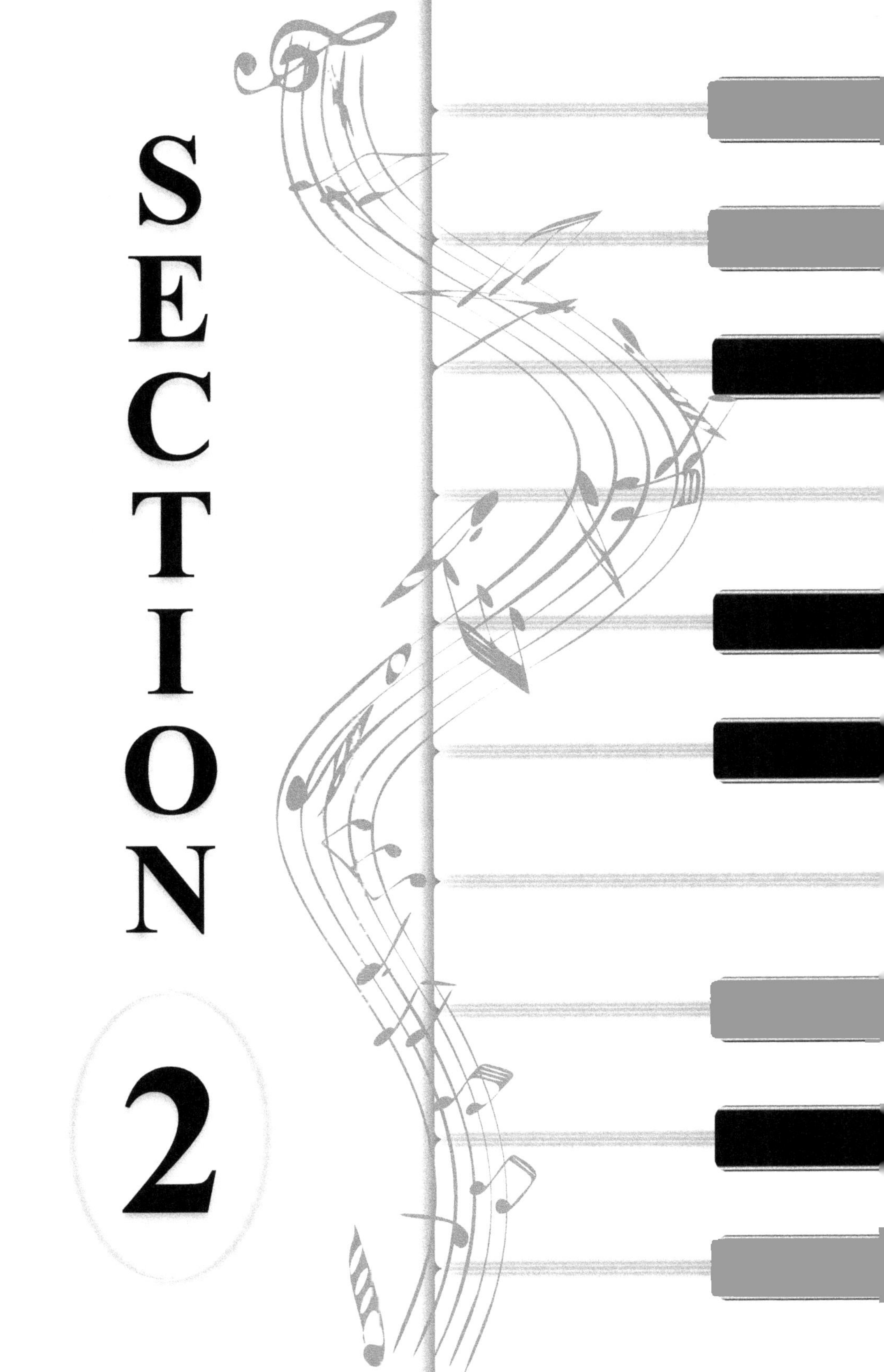
SECTION
2

The four steps to learning a new skill

The following 'Four Steps of Competence' was developed by Gordon Training International and their employee Noel Burch in the 1970s. I have used it many times when training people for an understanding of the learning process. There are 4 steps to learning a new skill. They are, from the bottom step…

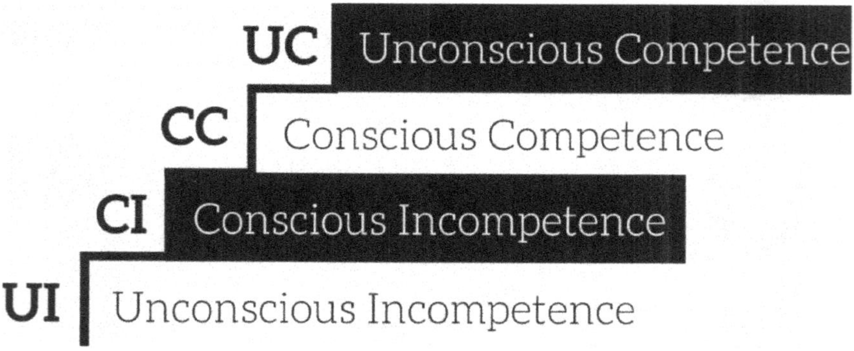

1. Unconscious Incompetence (UI)
2. Conscious Incompetence (CI)
3. Conscious Competence (CC)
4. Unconscious Competence (UC)

It is good to know where you are on the four steps to learning as it determines how you are feeling and the likelihood of you 'giving up' or staying the course.

Step 1: Unconscious Incompetence. You are right at the very beginning. You have just started to learn something and you do not know what you do not know. That is, you are unaware of all the things you need to know in order to learn the new skill. At this stage your motivation is intact and you may be excited by the journey ahead. You are looking forward to the learning process and the journey to mastery. We all have different preferences when it comes to learning and it can be helpful to know how you learn best. Some of us learn best when someone shows us (visual) some of us like to listen (audio) and some like to be hands-on (kinaesthetic). Video has taken off on the internet because so many people are visual learners. Others prefer to listen to podcasts or read transcripts and some people prefer to just roll up their sleeves and get on with it. I am a member of the last group. I learn best by doing. Because of that I didn't enjoy my time at school where I was forced to sit, watch and listen for most of the day. Think about how you learn best and use that to your advantage.

Step 2: Conscious Incompetence. At this stage you now have an understanding of what you need to know and you are very aware of your incompetence. This is the stage where frustration is high. It is also the stage where confidence wanes, motivation drops and people quit and give up. One of the problems is we watch people performing at a very high level and we compare ourselves to them. Please don't

do that! They were once at the beginning too. The only difference between you and them is time spent on the task. Listen to your self-talk! Be aware of things you are saying to yourself. If it is things like "I am useless" or "I will never get this" then it is a good idea to change what is being said. Try something else like, "I will get this" or "I am improving every day" and "If I just stick with it success is inevitable". For the most part we stop doing the things in life that we say we want because of poor self-talk. Improve your self-talk and your whole life will improve. There are a million books written on this subject so I won't elaborate any more here. For mine good self-talk equals good life. It is good to be aware that this stage will happen. Know that when you are feeling frustrated, confused and angry that it is normal. Everyone goes through this on the way to mastery. Being aware of it is the first step to overcoming it. When you are feeling those emotions just described it is best to stop and walk away. Go and find something else to do or sleep on it and come back to it the next day. It is amazing what a change can do for you.

Step 3: Conscious Competence. Now we are getting somewhere. You are having success, showing some skill and enjoying your results. Now you can put things together in a way that satisfies. However it still takes a lot of conscious effort. You have to concentrate and think about what you are doing. There is a conscious effort involved but it is a big step up from the frustration of Step 2. You are in a much happier space.

Step 4: Unconscious Competence. Eureka! You have made it. You now have muscle memory. Muscle memory is the concept that muscle-related tasks are much easier to perform after a certain amount of repetitions. Even if the task has not been performed for some time it is as if the muscles 'remember'. One of the most amazing moments in my keyboard playing was the day I found I could go from one chord to another without needing to look at the keyboard. (Something I still struggle with on the computer keyboard.) In unconscious competence you no longer have to work so hard. Things flow with far less effort and enjoyment is at its peak. At this level you are able to 'play' with what you are doing. This is where innovation and new discoveries are born. This is the level of mastery.

Key learnings

- Frustration will cause you to want to quit
- Monitor and adjust self-talk to increase motivation and lessen the risk of quitting
- When frustration gets high, stop. Go and do something else
- Know that it is a journey and results do not happen instantly

"The only thing between you and
mastery is time..."
Christopher Lavery

How to Practise

Please read this before you go any further.

I have decided to place this chapter here before explaining how to find and play scales, chords and all the rest of it. How you practise is most important for obtaining fast results. When teaching people to juggle I have noticed an impatience in many to get the end result. By that I mean they want to juggle three balls and they want to do it now! There is an unwillingness by many to put in the groundwork first and work with one ball, get that, work up to two balls, then finally take on three, four, five and more. A house built on poor foundations will not stand strong for any length of time. The same thing happens when I teach people how to twirl sticks and poi. Everyone wants to go fast and 'look good' before they have done the basics. When it comes to sticks and poi this can result in some nasty reminders that you are not ready yet when you hit yourself in the back of the head, the shin or in the case of males in the 'goolies'. Ouch! Some of them do it with fire waaaay before they are ready with nasty results.

Fortunately the learning of the keyboard should not result in any nasty injuries. However the same principles apply. Patience is the key.

Trying to play a piece at full speed when you are not ready, just results in a lot of mistakes and a feeling that I am not good enough.

You are definitely good enough. It is just a matter of time.

The way you practise is just as important as how often and how long you practise. Be aware it will take a while to get your fingers in shape (especially older fingers) but remember I didn't begin until I was 40 and I couldn't stretch my fingers an octave (that is from one C to the next C) when I began. So take it easy. Get it right. Music still sounds good played slowly (think slow classical piece or slow blues). However… ***It doesn't sound good if you are hitting the wrong notes.***

Here is the rule I adopted from my mentor Duncan Lorien. If you are playing a scale or a piece of music and you make a mistake? Slow it down by half and play it again at half the speed you were playing it the first time. Play it three times at a slower speed making sure you hit all the notes perfectly as you bring it back up to speed. It is very important that you do this even if you feel it is tedious. If you continue to play at the speed you have you will most likely continue to make the same mistake over and over and build that mistake into everything you do. Everything becomes habit so…

Make sure you are building good habits – not poor habits.

You may have heard the analogy of riding a bicycle? It is said that once you learn you never forget. I think this applies to all sorts of skills that we learn throughout life and playing an instrument is no different. Practise is the key to success in any field and gaining mastery over the keyboard is no exception. To gain maximum benefit one must make practise a consistent and daily habit and in order for that to happen you *must* have your instrument set up and ready to go and in a place that will be easy to access and use. You will never be able to get the daily practice required if you have your instrument packed away and have to unpack and set up every time you want to play. So regardless of whether it is a keyboard or a bassoon have the instrument set up and ready to go at all times so that you can practise *at any time*.

It is not always possible to practise at the same time every day, life will get in the way, but if it is set up and ready to go you can go for it whenever you have a spare five minutes and happen to be in that area. This brings us to an important point. How long should you practise for? The answer I usually give is…

Practise at least five minutes per day.

Everyone can find five minutes in their busy schedule. And usually if you sit down for five minutes you will stretch it and take some more. Many people will tell you that is not enough however I have found it is not the length that is important as much as the *daily* time spent. This is especially important in the early stages as you are cementing so many things in your mind and body (body memory) that you need to build upon your learnings every day. Once you have practised something a lot and you 'have it' it is unlikely you will ever lose it.

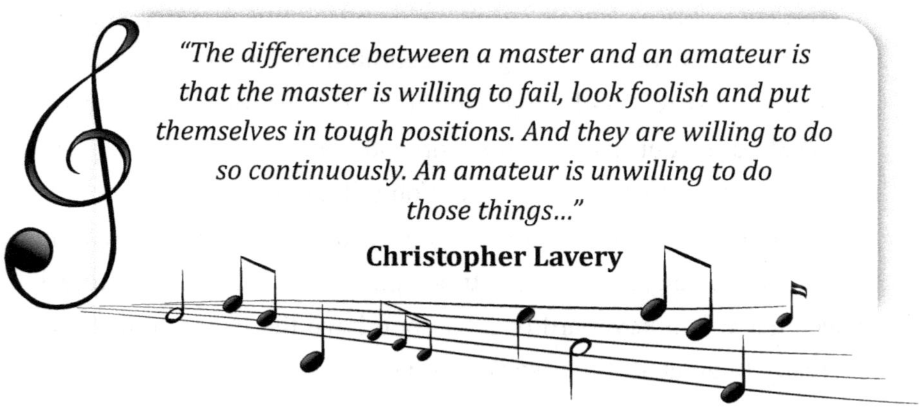

It is also important that your practice space is isolated from other people. That means you need to be able to close a door between you and others in your household because regardless of how 'good' you think you sound and how encouraging they might be you *will* drive people crazy if they have to listen to you during the early stages of you learning an instrument. (This is especially relevant if you are learning violin, brass, woodwind etc.) One of the great things about a keyboard is that you can plug in a set of headphones so that no one else has to listen to you practise.

The world's foremost cellist, Pablo Casals, is 83. He was asked one day why he continued to practise four and five hours a day. Casals answered, "Because I think I am making progress."

I am lucky as when I was first learning saxophone I had a house to myself during the day as other members of the household went off to work. Later when I moved in with the woman who was to become my wife we were caretaking an old church property that was to be turned into a golf course and there just happened to be an old church on the property. Great acoustics in churches and she didn't have to listen to me. How's that? I had the use of a church as my music room. You may not have a church or even an empty house but find a space you can call yours for the time you set for practice.

Most people are willing to practise the things they are already good at but not so happy to practice the things that challenge them. Practise that is ad hoc and erratic will not give the results required.

Key Learnings

- Make practice a daily habit – at least five minutes *every* day
- Have your instrument set up and ready to go
- Isolate yourself from others and practice in private
- Go for accuracy not speed

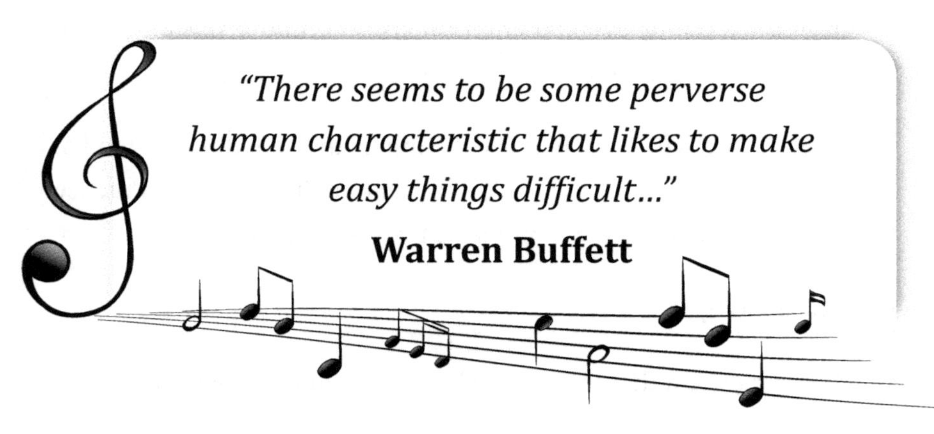
"There seems to be some perverse human characteristic that likes to make easy things difficult..."
Warren Buffett

Scales made easy

Scales. They are the bane of a young musician's life. We've all seen shows on TV or in the movies where a young person is being forced to practise their scales. It's almost a form of punishment. Scales are the melody part of music and in fact the word scale means *ladder* or *series of steps*. The space between the notes is called an interval. Intervals are used a lot in music and they have a series of dazzling and confusing names. Just to add to the confusion most intervals have two or three names. All you really need to know is that intervals are the spaces between notes. Scales are not something we use a lot when playing popular music, unless you are a playing lead breaks on guitar or other instrument.

Scales have rules, certain notes in a scale are considered more relevant and important than others. These are the *keynote*, which is the root or the *1st* note in the scale, the subdominant or 4th note and the dominant, the 5th note. We shall talk more about the 1, 4 and 5 a bit later. Generally the rules of scales say that you mostly play the notes of the scale but very occasionally throw in a note that isn't part of that scale. Playing mostly the notes of the scale keeps it agreeable and predictable and throwing in an outside note occasionally keeps it interesting.

Traditionally it is very difficult to learn scales as you are taught to learn and memorise every note in every scale. They don't teach you the simple pattern behind them.

Here we are going to learn the patterns for the most used scales. That is good news as this way you can learn one pattern and know 12 scales at once. I am going to say that again as it is such a departure from what is usually taught.

Learn one pattern and you learn 12 scales.

This is awesome news. It means you save countless hours compared to the grind of having to learn and memorise every note in every scale. This is the reason so many people give up music. It is also the reason so many musicians have a limited repertoire. Such a tedious *old school* way to learn. So learn the pattern and you can play with them all. No more boring and tedious repetition. That is unnecessary.

Scales are actually fun things to play with and explore. They give you the melodies and tunes we all enjoy so much. I spent years exploring scales and still marvel at their beautiful simplicity. Combined with their matching chords you can spend hours and hours exploring, meandering and traversing these pathways.

Every type of scale is built on the same pattern.

In other words every Major scale contains the exact same pattern.

Every minor scale has the exact same pattern.

Every blues scale has the exact same pattern.

And so on through every scale and mode that has ever been. When you know these patterns you can quickly and easily work out and play any and every scale that exists of that particular type, whether it is C, D, F#, or B. (B is considered the "hardest" of scales as it uses all of the black keys… whoa!)

If you know the pattern for Major scales you can play *EVERY* Major scale.

If you know the pattern for minor scales you can play *EVERY* minor scale.

If you know the pattern for blues scales you can play *EVERY* blues scale, etc., etc., etc.

This also applies to *any* musical instrument. First, more good news. Compared to many other instruments…

The keyboard is laid out in a way that makes it incredibly easy and straight-forward to find everything.

One key follows another in a logical sequence so it is easy to find any note you need. And it is easy to step up and down the keyboard. This is not the case on other instruments. On a saxophone or a clarinet to find certain notes you have to consult a manual or a fingering chart and they may also require your fingers to twist into unnatural positions and angles.

The space between the notes is known as an interval and is called a semi-tone or a half-step (or in our example '1', one space) when moving from one note to the next we say we are moving a semi-tone or a half-step. When we are moving two spaces on the keyboard we are moving a tone or a whole step (or '2'spaces). Why are there two different names? Because one is the European system and one system developed in America and is the American system – just another little thing to confuse new players to music.

As easy as 1, 2, 3, 4.

Here is the good news, if you can count up to four and you can easily learn any scale that ever existed, in fact most scales are a heck of a lot easier than that. To make it simple when moving from one note to the note next to it (whether it be black or white) we are moving one space or interval, counting by one. To take that a step further you can learn to count by twos, threes and even four and more. Start to look at the keyboard as a series of numbers. The amazing thing is that most music is written in only two scales. Those are the Major and minor scales. Over 98% of Western music is written in these two scales. So if you learn a couple of patterns for scales and a couple of chord patterns you have pretty much got it covered. So now let's have a look at these patterns.

Once again I refer to Duncan Lorien and The Understanding of Music Seminar™ where Duncan teaches that the easiest way to learn scales on the keyboard is to learn the patterns for the spaces between the notes rather than the notes themselves.

Below is the most popular pattern of them all. The Major scale. By the way it is called the Major scale because it is the scale that is used most often. The pattern is…

2, 2, 1, 2, 2, 2, 1

To play this scale, place the right thumb (I have named the thumb '0' in the diagram below) of your right hand on a note. (For simplicity perhaps start on a 'C' as traditional music teaches, as all of the notes in the scale are white. The C is also the most played note, scale and chord in music. It is pretty important and central to the whole thing both historically and in contemporary times.)

Now move up two, move up two, move up one, move up two, move up two and move up one, landing you back on the same note you started on. This is also called an *octave,* meaning eight. You have just played eight notes from one C to the next C. This applies to all the notes on the keyboard. Going from one note to the next note of that type is called an octave.

For the C Major scale place your right thumb on a C and then going up the keyboard play every white note until you hit the next C. Practise going back down the scale as well, back to where you started. The C Major scale is very easy as you are simply playing all the white notes. This is also the first scale you will learn in conventional teaching as well as it is considered the *easiest* scale. As you are playing this scale I want you to notice that you are playing the above pattern. I also want you to notice the 'sound' of this scale. This is the scale made famous

by Julie Andrews in the movie *The Sound of Music*. Remember Do, Re, Me, Fa, So La Te, Do? If you have ever watched this movie you will have the sound of this scale firmly planted in your mind. Sing it as you play it. Become very familiar with how it sounds. The reason is because if you ever play a "wrong" note you will instantly recognise it. And if you have never watched *The Sound of Music* then I highly recommend you get a copy and find the time to do so.

2, 2, 1, 2, 2, 2, 1

The diagram shows the Major scale starting on the C and a second Major scale beginning on the B. The '0' is your thumb or starting note.

So you can see a C Major scale and a B Major scale.

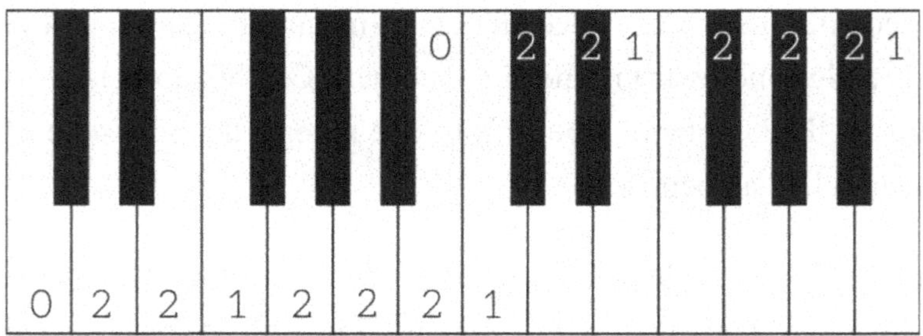

Plant the scale in your head memorise it and then start to practise placing your thumb on a different note and *play the pattern*. Remember that you are counting each note. Each white note *and* each black note. Be careful not to get tricked at the B and C and E and F where there is no black note.

When playing the scale *listen* very carefully. This is the do, re, mi, fa, so, la, te, do, scale so when you play this scale that is what you should hear. When you play it with a different starting note it will still sound the same. It will sound higher or lower but it will sound the same. So if you do hit a false note your ear will tell you immediately.

Simple so far? I hope it soon becomes very, very simple to count by two and one, up and down the keyboard.

So that is the major part of music covered. Literally.

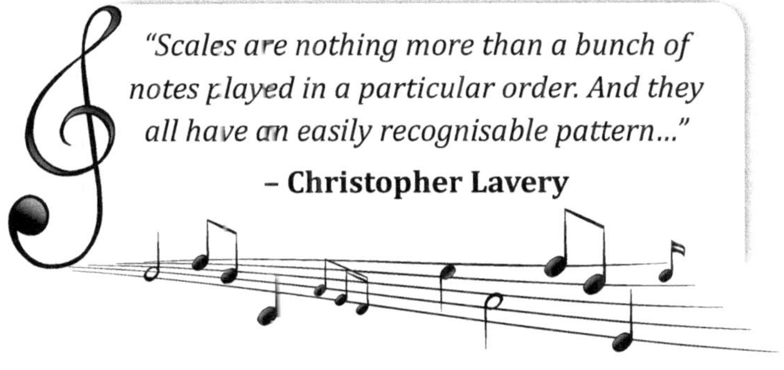

Now let's look at the minor scale.

2, 1, 2, 2, 1, 2, 2

Repeat the above steps as applied to the Major scale. Find a note to start on. (may as well be the 'C' or if you want to start on all white notes try the relative minor of the 'C' which is 'A') Move up two, move up one, move up two, move up two, move up one, move up

two, and move up two. Remember you should land on the same note you started on. Listen carefully to the sound of the scale as when you start on a different note (otherwise known as changing key) it should sound the same, just higher or lower.

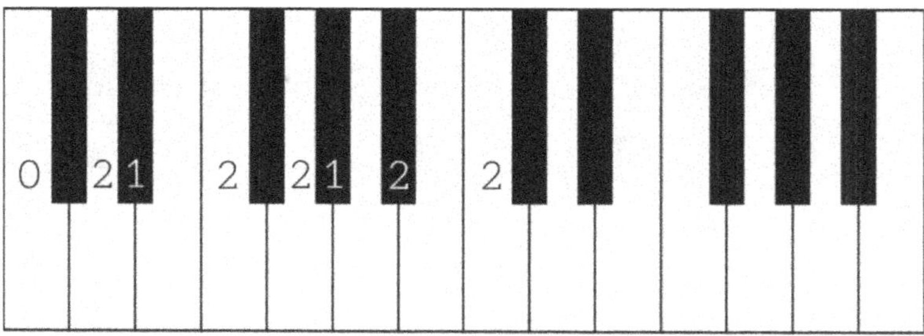

Now for those wanting to venture a little further down the rabbit hole let the fun begin.

Here we have a blues scale.

3, 2, 1, 1, 3, 2

This scale needs you to move three spaces… twice… whoa! Can you handle it?

Once again start on any key. Count up three, count up two, count up one, count up one, count up three and count up two.

This scale is actually used in a lot of popular styles, not just blues but in rock and roll and more.

There is also other ways to play the blues that do not require the blues scale. As they say the blues is a *feeling* not a method.

Here's the blues scale in 'C':

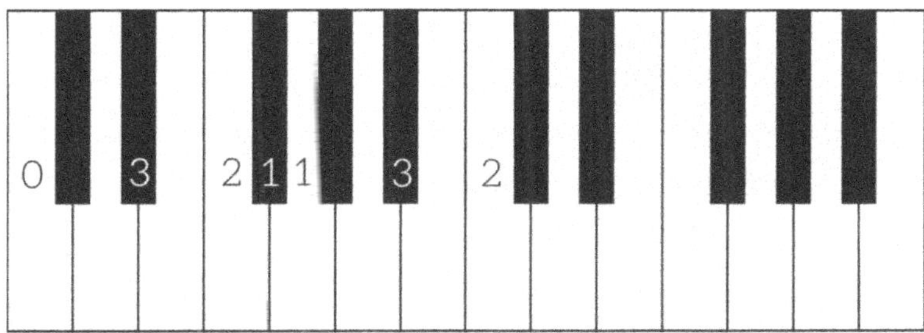

It amazes me as I surf the internet there seems to be a huge demand for learning how to play the blues. So many methods offered, so many *secrets* revealed. Remember this... the blues was born out of the cotton fields by a bunch of people who had little in the way of money or resources. The original players were simple and largely uneducated people who found a means of expression with what they had. By its very nature it is unsophisticated and thus easy. If you have an interest in this form of music I would suggest that you spend a bit of time playing with the scale. It is generally only played in a limited number of keys those being C, D, E, A and G. Most musicians avoid the black notes/keys. Why is that? Because musicians must learn each scale individually and they just never get to the ones that use a lot of black keys.

Here is a suggestion for you. Try the blues scale in E flat. You will find that this scale uses all of the black keys and only one white key and is indeed very simple to play.

But don't worry about it too much because very few other musicians will be able to play it with you.

So we have now learned three of the most popular scales that are commonly used; the Major scale, the minor scale and the blues scale.

It is interesting to note that each Major scale has a related minor scale. C Major for example uses the same notes as A minor i.e., all the white notes. Only the start and finishing positions vary. C Major starting on the C and A minor starting on the A. To find the related minor of any Major just count down three keys/notes/semitones or half steps and bingo there it is. There are other relationships between the notes, scales and chords that will be revealed as we move through the book.

Duncan Lorien teaches that if you come across a scale that someone shows you or you find on a website or music book, then take note of the pattern inherent in that scale and you can

Key Learnings

- A scale is a series of notes played in a particular pattern
- All scales have a pattern
- Learn one pattern and you learn 12 scales
- Scales start and finish on a particular note i.e. a C scale starts and finishes on a C
- Any scale type shares the same pattern e.g., a Major scale has the same pattern regardless of whether it's in C, F sharp or B flat. All minor scales have the same pattern.
- Scales can be fun

"A chord is simple. It is any three (or more) notes played together..."
Christopher Lavery

Chords made easy

Major and minor chords (mostly all you need)

Chords are magical things. Chords are like the meat and potatoes of music. They are the basis of most popular music and also contain the melodies and the variations that keep it all interesting and entertaining. When you know and understand chords you have the whole musical world at your fingertips. You can truly communicate using the language and art of music.

Once again we enter a space that a lot of people find confusing and frustrating. And of course the music establishment like to keep it that way. Chords, just like scales have patterns. And there are rules to those patterns. Once again we find that any chords of a group e.g., major chords, all share the same pattern. And once again if you know that pattern then you can work out and play any chord from that group. Learn the pattern and you learn 12 chords. So even though they may look different and require different fingerings, in reality there is no difference between say a C major chord and a G sharp Major chord, they are exactly the same and use exactly the same pattern.

As with scales, Duncan Lorien teaches in The Understanding of Music Seminar™ the easiest way to learn chords on the keyboard is to learn the patterns for the spaces between the notes rather than the notes themselves.

We will start by looking at the pattern for Major chords. Major chords are sometimes referred to as 'happy' chords. Generally they have an uplifting sound that makes people feel good.

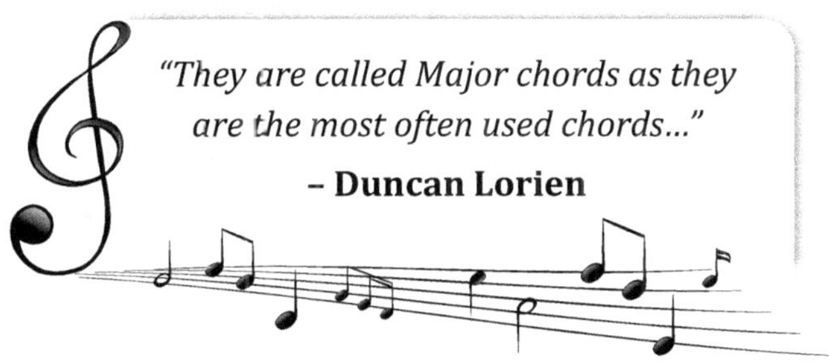

Here is the pattern for Major chords.

4, 3

The diagram below shows a C Major chord and a C# Major chord

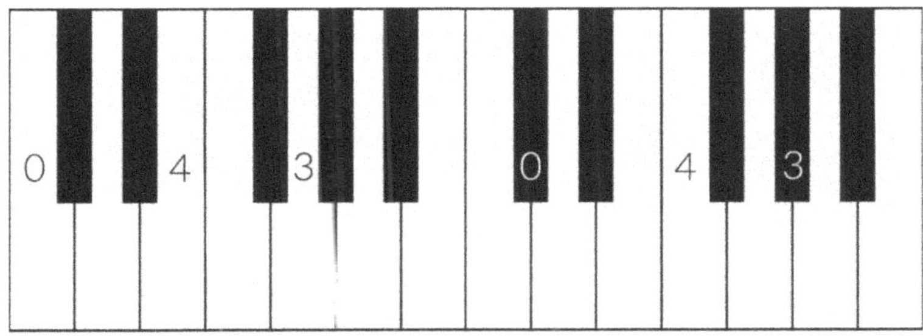

That is it. Looks pretty easy doesn't it? And it is. However it does take a bit of consistent practice before you can grab any chord quickly and easily.

As previously mentioned a chord is made up of at least three notes that harmonise nicely together and are played in a particular pattern.

The numbers 4 and 3 are the spaces or intervals between the notes and between your fingers. So with your right hand place a finger or thumb on any key. Count up 1, 2, 3, 4 (counting black and white keys) place a finger on that note, then count up 1, 2, 3 (black and white) and place a finger on that note. Play those notes together and you have a Major chord. Hey presto! Musical Magic!!

Try it on the C first. Count up 4 and you will find the E, count up 3 and you will find the G. Have a look at the diagram below. The note you play with your thumb is known as the root or keynote. Below you can see the C Major chord and the C# Major chord. By moving each finger up or down one in the same direction you will find the next chord. It doesn't take long using this method to discover all the Major chords.

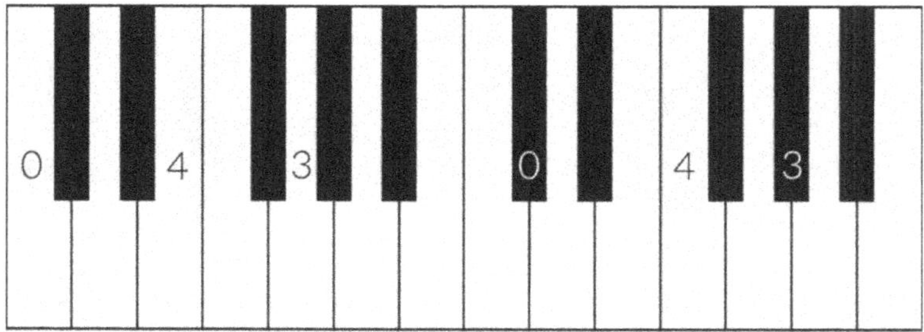

Try playing the keynote with your left hand as you play the chord. So if you are playing the C chord with your right hand find and play a bass C (a lower C to the left side of the keyboard) with your left hand. Mostly keyboard players only play bass notes with their left hand

and a lot of music only calls for this to happen, often using only your pinky, index finger and thumb. The 1, 4 and 5 on your left hand.

The question also arises as to what fingers 'should' use when playing chords. Traditionally you use thumb, middle finger and pinky (the 1, 3 and 5 fingers) to play a three note chord and these are probably the best to use if you can. Me? I say use whatever you are comfortable with or indeed have. (I don't use the "normal" fingers, I use thumb, index and ring finger – the 1, 2 and 4 – but no one told me which ones I should be using) Not everyone has full use of their fingers or even has all their fingers, so *use whatever you find comfortable and easiest for you.*

Something to notice when you are finding and playing chords is this... most related chords use the same fingering pattern. Play a C, F and G and you will see you can lock your fingers and play each chord. You will find the same thing happens when you play an A, D and E. This also works with minor chords, chords that use black notes and when playing related scales. Lock your fingers in the position for one and it is locked and loaded to play the others. Cm, Fm and Gm. Am, Dm and Em. C#, F# and G#. The odd chord out is B. I will make a video to cover the similar fingering and put it up on the website.

The most commonly played chords in music are the C, F and G. So go ahead and locate those three chords. As you play each chord with your right hand also play the bass note with your left hand. So as you play the C chord find and play a C to the left of centre. Remember middle C? Here is where it comes in handy. Move to the F chord and also

play a low F note and likewise with the G, play the chord and play the bass note. How you play with the left hand is up to you and your left hand resources but generally you would play the C with your pinky, the F with your index finger and the G with your thumb.

Remember all of this is available as video instruction on the website. If you are struggling to understand these concepts or

It is also a good idea to find the chord with your left hand as well. Learn to find and play the chord with *both* hands. (To find left hand chords you would place your pinky on the first note count up 4, place your middle finger on that note, then count up 3 and place your thumb on that note. You can play the whole chord with one hand and the notes of the chord with the other. Initially you might find doing this extremely challenging as your fingers will only work a certain way, but over time, and with practice, you will be able to play however you want. You just have to make the connections between your fingers and your brain and make them do what you are asking. This takes practise. It takes pushing through the Conscious Incompetence stage of the learning process, not being overwhelmed by the frustration of it and continuing to practise to reach the Consciously Competent and finally the Unconscious Competence of the master. I well remember the day when I realised I could play chords without needing to look at the keyboard. I was amazed and inspired and it just happened as a result of steady and consistent practice.

Having worked out the method for finding Major chords it now becomes very easy to find minor chords.

They are called 'minor' chords as they are used less often.

Here is the pattern for minor chords.

3, 4

Shown below is the C minor chord and the C# minor chord.

By moving *each* finger up or down *one* in the same direction you will find the next chord. It doesn't take long using this method to discover all the minor chords.

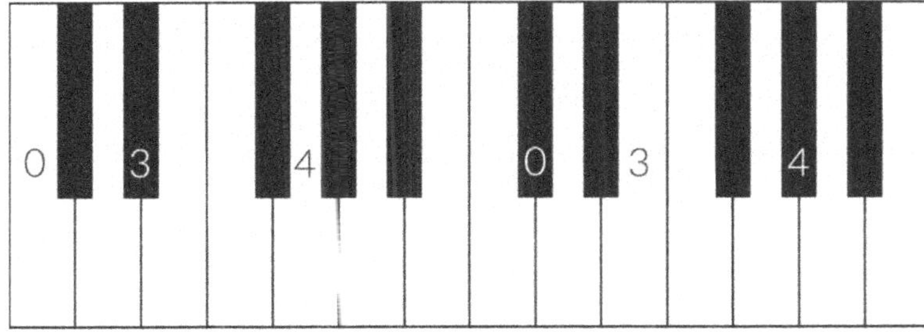

The same logic applies here as used previously. Place your thumb on a note and count up 3 notes (count both black and white) place a finger on that key and then count up 4 and do the same. Play all three notes together and you are playing the chord. Astute observers will notice the pattern for minor chords is very similar to the pattern for Major chords. Indeed the 'outside' fingers remain in the same positions. It is only the middle finger that changes by going down one key or note. So if you

are playing a Major chord you can also find and play a minor chord simply by moving your middle finger back one key. How good is that?!!

As with the scales, every Major chord has a related or relative minor chord and it is found in the same place each time. Down 3 notes or keys from the root note of the Major. So as with our example in the scales section, the relative minor chord of the C Major is an A minor. You will find the relative minor chord has only one note that is different from the Major version but the sound produced is markedly different. We will see how these chords go together nicely in the section on how songs are constructed further along in the book.

Chords can be played several different ways. You can play all the notes together as one. You can play the notes contained in the chord one at a time (this is what guitarists are doing when they are plucking the strings and other instruments such as brass and woodwind will play chords one note at a time) or you can play two notes and then one note. All of these methods produce a different sound and give you different possibilities. Practice each way to play the chord. Go to the website at and have a look at the "How to Play Chords" video.

I like to play chords with both hands. Usually one hand plays the full chord while the other plays the notes of the chord, so practise finding chords with both hands. If I am repeating myself it is because repetition is the mother of all learning. To find Major chords place your right thumb on any note, black or white, count up 4 and then count up 3. Play those 3 notes together and you have a Major chord. That chord is identified by the root note or keynote, that is, the note you have your thumb on. If your thumb is playing a C then you are playing a C Major chord. Your fingers will be on the E and the G.

Now try this… Move each finger up one, onto the C#, the F# and the G# and you will now have the C# Major chord. This is magic and a great way to learn ALL the Major chords. Simply start at any Major chord and by moving each finger up or down one you will find the next Major chord. Thus you can work your way up and down the keyboard finding and playing all the Major chords. Find the same chord with both hands and play the notes one at a time. Now move each finger up or down one. Do it slowly to be sure you are moving to the correct key. You are now playing the next chord up or down. Name it and practice it. Continue doing this until you have moved through the range from where you started and back again. This is an awesome way to learn all the chords and practice the fingering for them.

You can do the same thing with minor chords or any type of chord you wish to learn. You can alternate by playing Major chords and then minor chords. You can move your middle finger to change from the Major to the minor. Have fun with it, this is an exercise in discovery it should be fun and educational at the same time. Remember, find them, name them *and*… accuracy not speed.

Duncan Lorien teaches that if you come across a chord that someone shows you or you find on a website or music book, then take note of the pattern inherent in that scale and you can apply it to any key.

Key Learnings

- 'Major' means most often used
- 'Minor' means less often used
- The formula for Major chords is 4 3
- The formula for minor chords is 3 4
- Learn one pattern and you learn 12 chords
- Learn these 2 patterns and you can play 98% of Western music
- Use the fingers that feel most comfortable to you

"Whatever you can do or dream you can, begin it. Boldness has genius, power and magic in it. Begin it now..."
Johann Wolfgang von Goethe

More easy chords – 7ths, 2nds, 4ths, 6ths and more

There are a few other commonly used chords that we will cover here so that you can find them easily. Namely *7ths* or dominant 7th chords, suspended chords, (suspended 2nds and suspended 4ths) and other numbered chords and intervals. Firstly let's deal with the dominant 7th/7th chords. (Why can't they just have *one* name for everything?!!)

Have a look at the diagram below.

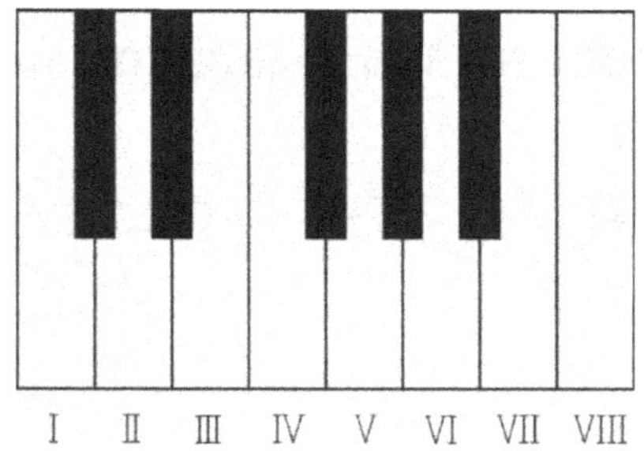

This diagram uses roman numerals. That should give you a clue as to how old it is. Although it may be a bit cool and add mystique to the process it is not helpful and nor is it particularly accurate. As you can see the keys are numbered I-II-III-IV-V-VI-VII-VIII. 1 being the keynote (or root) then up the keys through 2, 3, 4, 5 and so forth. This is great because it (often but not always) makes it easy to find other types of chords e.g., C2, C4, C6, C9. Using your numbered fingers will let you work out up to 5 easily and quickly and then a quick count to find the other numbers up and down the keyboard (remember the octave or next C up the keyboard is 8, this helps when you are looking for a C11 or higher) The reason it is confusing and inaccurate is because this is a system that was developed and used prior to the black notes being added to the keyboard. It is totally based on the C Major scale so it doesn't allow or take into account the black notes.

What the..? (I hope by now you are getting a clue as to why music is difficult and confusing.) So you can use this system to find some 7ths but not all 7ths For example, C7. So what did they come up with to allow for the exceptions? Nothing. Or at least not something that makes a lot of sense and is not totally confusing to the average student of music. You just have to know which ones have a black note. (Which means you need a teacher and lots of expensive lessons). You may sometimes see it written this way I- #II- III-#IV-V-VI-bVII – no confusion there right?

Fortunately there is a way to accurately find the 7th and it's not very difficult at all.

The seventh note for any keynote is two notes down from that keynote

In other words find the keynote and count down two notes (counting black and white) and that note is your 7th. Using our C-F-G example if you count down 2 from the C you will land on the B♭. Try this with other notes and you will quickly find the 7th of every note. Add that note to the chord and *voila* you have a dominant 7th chord which is usually written on a chord chart as C7.

The diagram below shows the finger numbering system used for learning piano keyboard.

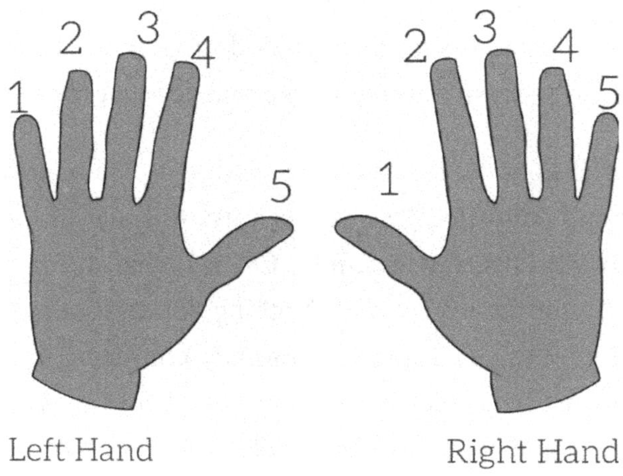

This numbering system can be very handy for learning chords and chord progressions. The following is a little trick I picked up from Tim Gross on www.pianogenius.com, who like Duncan uses a numbering system to get people playing quickly and easily. Look at the diagrams above with the numbered fingers and see the one below with our numbered fingers placed on the keyboard. You will see the fingers and the numbers line up with the Roman numerals and give us our sus2 and sus4 chords. The no 4 chord is also just called a suspended chord and may be written as Csus, Cs4 or Csus4 whereas the no 2 chord is always called a suspended second and will be written as C2sus, Cs2 or Csus2. Yes it is all very sus and I hope this is making sense. It is blindingly obvious once you use this system it makes finding these chords so very easy.

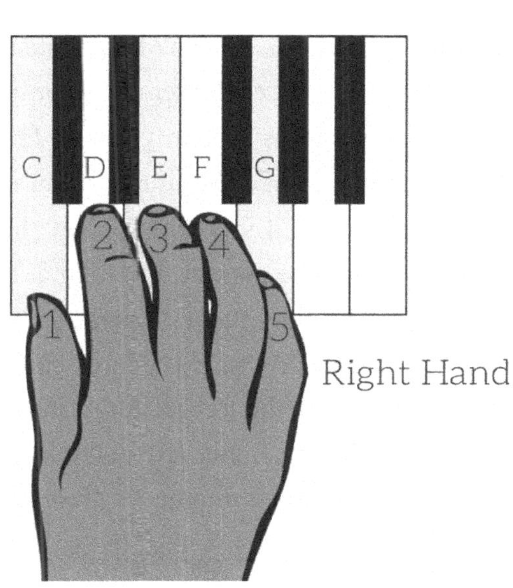

When it comes to chords we have our basic unit which is the Major chord (remember Major means *most often used*). Most other chords you need are a variation on the Major chord. The root or thumb never changes and mostly the top note stays the same. If you need the minor chord then move your middle finger back one note. If you want a sus2nd play the note under your 2nd finger and likewise if you want a 4th (or sus chord) play the note under your fourth finger. Easy? Looking at the chart it is not difficult to deduce that if you want a 6th or 7th then they can be found by counting up from your 5th finger and playing the relevant note.

Now you are moving your top finger or adding the extra note to the major chord. Sometimes a piece requires you to play a 13th (written as C13). Can you find it using this system? Indeed just keep counting up until you land on the 13th note. Remember it only applies to the white notes but usually using this system you will find the note you are seeking. Simply replace or add the number you require. So if a chord chart calls for a C2 or a C4 you play the key that is under that finger. In most cases you will be correct. Looking at the chart above if you need a C2 you would play the 1, 2 and 5. If you need a C4 you would play the 1, 4 and 5. These two chords can also be used to spice up a piece of music and make it more interesting by using them instead of the Major chord. Remember an octave is 8 notes up from the keynote and this can help when finding a C9 for example.

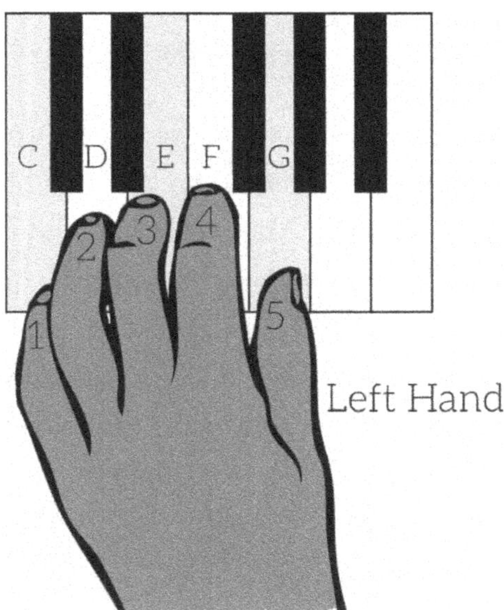

This section can be confusing as we now have two numbering systems to think about. The Lorien system I first introduced you to which involves counting all the keys, black and white, up and down the keyboard and the ancient system of numbering which uses roman numerals and is based on the C Major scale and so only counts the white notes. I don't wish to muddy the waters by introducing another system but this one is the one that musicians and music books speak so it is important to know so that you understand what they are talking about. If you are playing in C then it can be very useful but in other keys you may need to go back to counting the keys. Use whichever is easiest for you.

Key learnings

- Chords are easy
- All chords have a pattern
- Chords contain three or more notes
- Learn the pattern for one chord and you learn 12 chords
- You only need to move one finger to go from a Major chord to a minor chord to a sus2 or sus4
- All chords have related chords
- There is a numbering system that uses roman numerals and is based on the C Major scale that only counts white notes

"All things are difficult before they are easy..."
Thomas Fuller

Chord inversions

'Inverting' a chord allows you to play that chord three different ways. There is the standard chord or 'root' position, the first inversion and the second inversion. Same chord, played three different ways. Why would you want to do that? Playing an inversion (aka an inverted chord) makes it easier to move your fingers from one chord to the next chord. So rather than lifting your fingers off the keyboard and moving your whole hand up or down the keys to get to the next chord, you are able to go from one chord to the next using less movement. Efficiency experts would love chord inversions.

In most cases you can leave one finger in place and move two of your other fingers. This makes it much easier to play and much quicker and more efficient. Let's have a look at what chord inversions look like and how they can be used to make playing easier.

In our standard 1-4-5 pattern we will have the keynote chord (C), the dominant chord (F) and the subdominant chord (G). Using the C-F-G example once more, if we are playing the chords in the 'normal' or 'root' position we would have to go from the C to the F by lifting our hand off the keyboard and moving the whole pattern up to the F position. We would also do the same thing to find the G chord.

However, observant people will notice that, the C chord and the F chord share the note C and the C chord and the G chord share the note G. That is, the C Major chord is made up of C, E and G, the F Major

chord is made up of F, A and C and the G Major chord is made up of G, B and D. So to go from a C Major chord to an F Major chord we can leave our thumb on the C and move two fingers up to the F and the A. Now if you hold that pattern and move it up one you will also find the G major chord playing D, G and B. Same chords – minimum movement.

Check out the diagram below. Here we have a C Major chord containing C, E and G. The first diagram shows it in its root position.

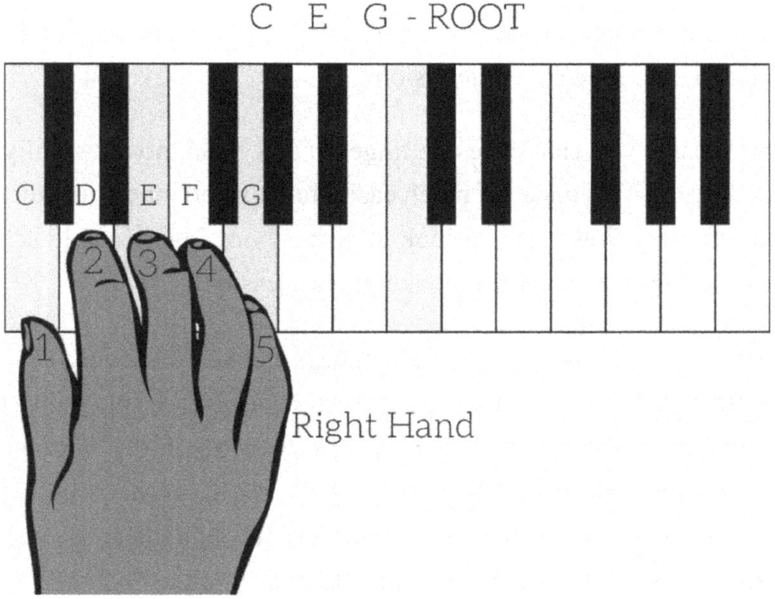

The first inversion has moved the C to the top position so now we are playing E, G and C.

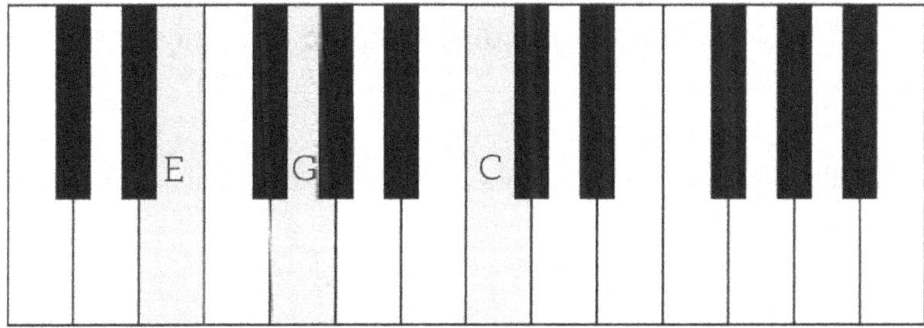

The second inversion moves the G to the bottom position so now we are playing G, C and E.

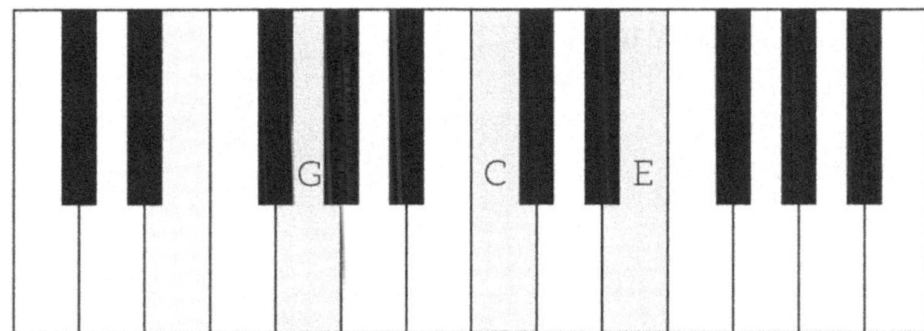

As your playing improves you will find it easy a lot of the time to move from one root position to another quickly and easily. However it is not always possible to do without creating an awkward gap in the music. When working out whether an inversion is needed I play the piece of music I am learning, and play all the chords in their root

position. I quickly find whether an inversion is needed and where. There are some chords that I always play as an inversion as they just fit better in most pieces of music or playing them in that position has just become a habit for me. There are no hard and fast 'rules' with inversions. Use them as required and use the ones most comfortable to you.

If you still find this confusing please go to the website and check out the video on inversions.

Key Learnings

- An inversion is a way of playing the same chord using different fingerings
- Inversions make it easier and quicker to play a piece of music
- Inversions are easy to learn

"It is easy to read a book and enjoy the knowledge. Knowledge is nice. What will it take for you to get up and take action...?"
Christopher Lavery

As easy as 1-4-5

This may be the most powerful section of this whole book.

If you get this concept then you open the door to being able to play most western music from the last hundred years. You will also be able to enjoy sitting down and improvising to your heart's content as this is *the* major pattern in western music.

It's used in pop music, blues music, rock n roll and just about every type of musical genre. This pattern is known as 1-4-5. We have already seen its application in the previous chapters. You may have seen or heard that all pop songs have been written in three chords and that you only need to know three chords in order to be able to play hundreds of pop songs. Whilst this is true, it's more true to say that they've all been written in the one pattern, that pattern being 1-4-5. So how does this transfer to the piano keyboard? Let me show how easy this is, exactly how this transfers to the keyboard and how you can take this pattern and overlay it on any key.

Hold up your right hand and number your fingers starting with the thumb as number one, index finger is number two, middle finger number three, ring finger is four and pinky is number five.

1 2 3 4 5

Right Hand

Now place your hand on the keyboard so that your fingers cover five consecutive white notes.

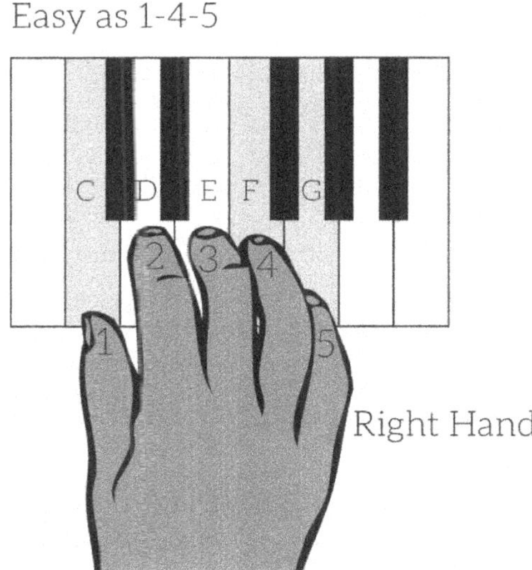

For this exercise find a C and place your thumb on the C. Your fingers should now cover the D, E, F and G.

Your thumb is on the number ONE. Your ring finger is on the number FOUR and your pinky is one the number FIVE. There it is. The key is in your hand and right under your fingertips. Note that this also works on your left hand.

This gives you the three main chords to use in any tune. In the above example it is C-F and G. These are the three most commonly used chords in all music. Move your thumb up to the G and you will discover the second most commonly used three chords, the G-C and D.

If you can find these three chords you can now play rock and roll, pop, blues, C&W and more. Or if you're wishing to write some tunes take note; this is incredibly powerful.

So logically if you move your fingers up one note you will now have your fingers sitting on the C#-F#-G#. Move them up one more and you have D-G-A.

Play with this. Place your thumb on any note and find the 1-4-5.

Note: If it doesn't "sound right" it probably isn't. Check your fingers.

Not to get too technical but the notes under 1-4-5 are known as…

ONE FOUR FIVE
the Keynote, the Dominant, the Subdominant.

Let's look at the example of C-F-G.

C is the keynote.

F is the dominant.

G is the subdominant.

You wanna play da blues? All you have to do is add the 7th to this combination and voila… instant blues. (Go to the website and see)

Now let's add another note to this pattern so that you have four chords in your toolbox. We've mentioned this note a couple of times already and it is known as the relative minor note. The relative minor is related to the keynote and is located three notes down from the keynote.

Once again our example of C-F-G.

C – is the keynote.

F – is the dominant.

G – is the subdominant.

Am – is the relative minor.

Every Major scale and chord has a relative minor scale and chord. For example the C Major scale uses the same notes as the A minor scale. That is, all the white notes. It is just the start and finishing points that change. C Major starts and finishes on a C whereas A minor starts and finishes on an A. Play those scales and you will discover a very different sound. The C Major chord shares the C and E with the A minor chord. You will note that the A minor is three notes down from the C Major. So now you can be assured that ***all*** the relative minor chords are to be found *three keys down* from their Major chord. So now we can add a minor chord to our three major chords.

Oh boy, when I got this, did my musical world expand. I have some videos on the website that show how useful this is please go and check them out.

A note on the 1-4-5 system. Remember, it was devised for the C Major scale back in the days of the Roman empire and so only works reliably on (most of) the white keys/notes and none of the black keys/notes. To find the dominant and subdominant of the F, B and all the black notes you can use the Dorien system of counting the spaces. You will find the subdominant, five keys up from your keynote or starting note, and the dominant seven keys up from the keynote. Practice doing this and you will very soon

Key Learnings

- The 1-4-5 pattern is the most prevalent pattern in music
- Learn this pattern and you can play the majority of popular music from the last hundred years
- Add the 7th for instant blues music
- Add the relative minor for interest and variation
- Learn this pattern and you can write your own songs with ease

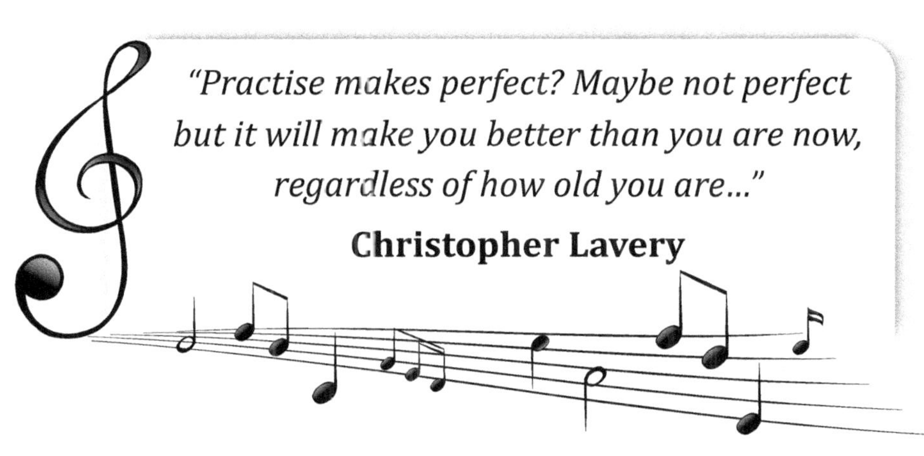
"Practise makes perfect? Maybe not perfect
but it will make you better than you are now,
regardless of how old you are..."
Christopher Lavery

Putting it together – Practise Part 2

We have covered what fingers you should use in a previous chapter. Traditionally you use thumb, middle finger and pinky to play a three note chord and these are probably the best to use if you can. Me? I say use whatever you are comfortable with or whatever you have available (I don't use the "normal" fingers, I use thumb, index and ring finger but no one told me which ones I should be using.) Not everyone has full use of their fingers or even has all their fingers, so use whatever you find easiest. Whatever works for you.

The question then arises what should I be practising? The short answer is, whatever you are finding the most difficult. Generally speaking once you've got something you've 'got it'. No need to continue practising something that is coming easily. It is locked into muscle memory and comes easily.

Typically a practice session would begin with some **warm-ups** to get your fingers working. Finger stretches are also a good idea. Crack your knuckles if you are so inclined.

I like to begin by playing white notes using my thumb and fingers slowly moving up and down the keyboard one note at a time and increasing in speed.

Remember… if you mess it up slow it down!

I then like to play the chromatic scale (all the notes black and white) up and down the keyboard.

To learn the chords choose a keynote (1), find its dominant (4) and its subdominant (5) and practice playing them. Throw in the relative minor and go around and around a few times.

By that I mean play a 12-bar progression and throw in the relative minor as well. This helps you become familiar with the patterns for *that particular key* and is great training. Also practise their inversions and work out the best way to go from one to the other.

I used to choose a blues scale and do the same thing. Play it in the first position then play the related scales the 4th and the 5th. Try playing a chord with your left hand and a scale with your right. Mix it up play different scales. Your practice sessions will help you find your niche the thing that really tickles your fancy and the direction you want to go. So explore and play. Use your imagination and have fun.

Have a look at the website and the videos on practice. One of the main things with practise is to mix it up and keep it interesting.

Key Learnings

- Use the fingers that feel comfortable and easy for you
- Practise what is difficult
- Keep your practice sessions interesting
- If you make a mistake slow it down to half speed and repeat four times
- Go where it takes you

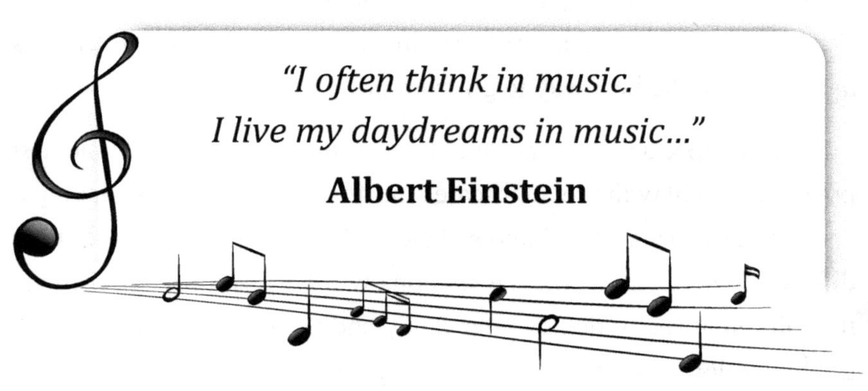
"I often think in music.
I live my daydreams in music..."
Albert Einstein

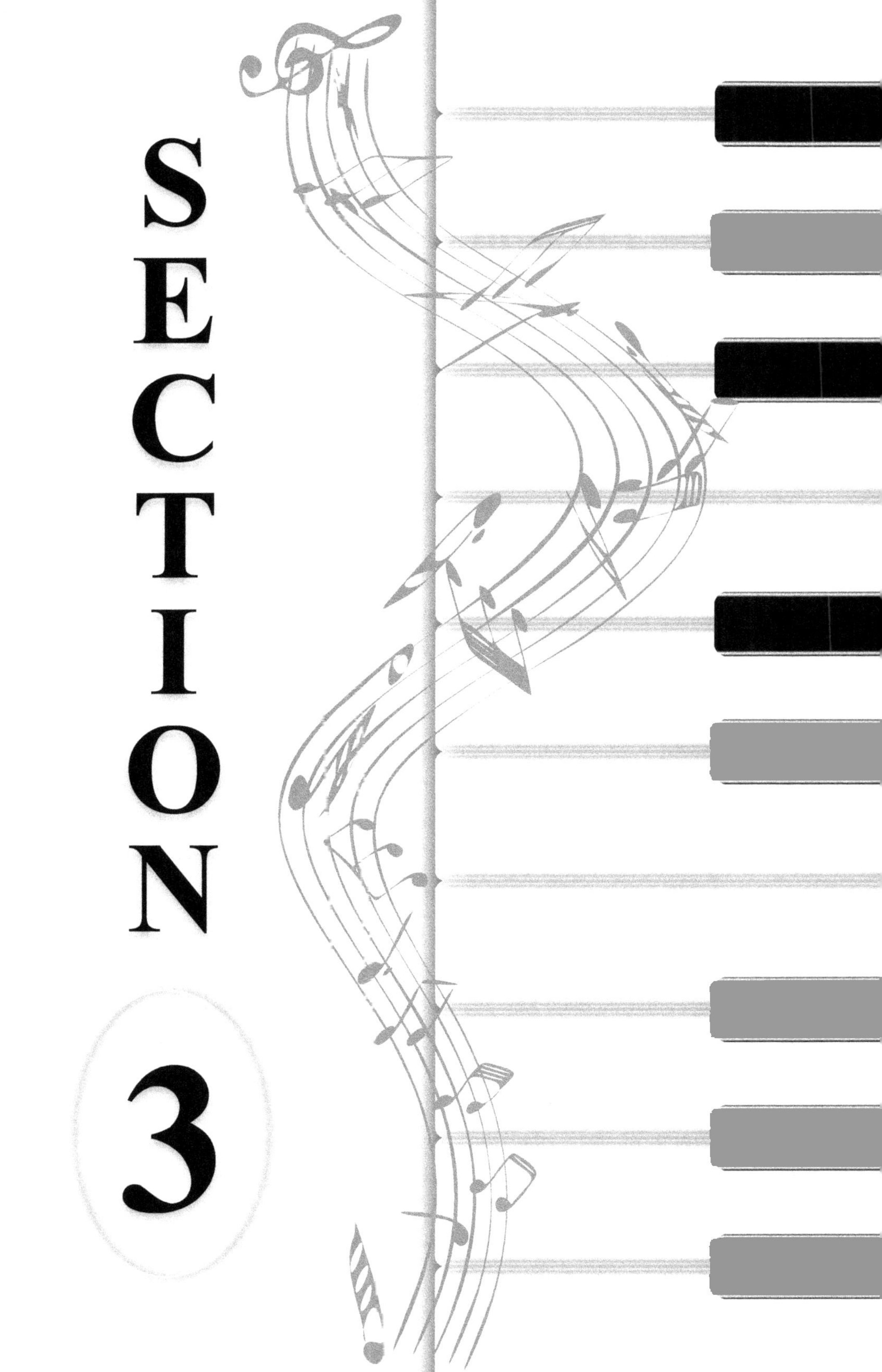
SECTION
3

Playing the blues

Since it seems that everyone wants to play the blues I thought I better jump on that bandwagon and show you how. Like many musical genres there are several styles of blues music which means there are lots of ways to play the blues. Many people will tell you that the blues is a 'feeling' rather than a method and there is some truth in that. For example there are no blues chords as such and you can play blues music using plain old Major chords… if you have the right 'feeling'. Usually blues uses a combination of Major and minor and very often, dominant 7th chords or just 7ths (usually written as C7). I explained how to find the dominant 7th in the chords made easy chapter and of course there is a video on the keyboard made easy website.

So you want to play blues? Here are a couple of easy methods to get you started. Once again my example is in C, so find the C minor chord and play the 1-4-5 chords, Cm, Fm and Gm. Throw in the Am to complete the circle. Mix them up with Major chords and see how it sounds. There are no hard and fast rules here. Decide what sounds good to you and play with it. Don't get stuck on the key of C either, play with this in all the keys. You will find you prefer certain keys over others and that each key has its own unique sound and style as is dictated by the positioning of their keys and the way you have to play them.

Another method is to play the dominant 7ths chords. The lovely discordant note that all blues lovers love is the 7th. Try this. Find the

C, F and G. (1-4-5) Now locate the 7ths for them (two down). Now play them one note at a time emphasising the 7th note. So play the C chord with the 7th (B♭), then the F with the 7th (E♭) and the G chord with its 7th (F). Mix it up, play with it and find the sound that you like the most. Play the note and the 7th only and see how that sounds.

And still a third method (based on key of C again). Find and play a C minor (Cm) chord. Hold the chord while you play the C blues scale with your right hand. (You can also use your foot pedal to hold the Cm.) Play an F chord (hold it) and repeat. Go between the Cm and the F on your left hand and play the C blues scale on your right hand. Add in other chords as you get the 'feel' for it. You can throw in a G or Gm, C7, Fm, Am – any of the chords related to C.

The 12-bar system...

I am a child of the 60's and 70's and as such I grew up on a steady diet of rock n roll, R n B and popular music. All of which use this 12-bar system. It is simple and easy so I include it here because I am all about simple and easy. Before I can go on and explain the 12-bar system we first need to understand what is a bar? I used to say the only bar I knew was a place to go and have a drink (even when I was playing in a band). Most of us know what it is simply because we have listened to so much music.

A bar is one count of four beats.

In other words if you count 1, 2, 3, 4 – that equals one bar. And what is a beat? Basically it is the speed of the count. I am not going to get into all the technicalities of this as I believe most people inherently know it from the amount of hours they have listened to music, tapped and clapped along with it, danced to it. We deal with it every day. Our heart beats a steady beat, motor cars, aeroplanes, washing machines, our steps on the pavement. We hear beats and rhythms all day every day. There are other variations on this but for our purposes here we are only going to deal with a 4-beat bar. How fast is that count of four? As fast as the particular piece of music is. Count it here…

1,2,3,4---1,2,3,4---1,2,3,4---1,2,3,4. Clap along, tap your foot, find the beat. Fortunately keyboards have built in metronomes (a thing that keeps the timing) and they have displays and they have in built rhythms. Learn to count the bars or 'feel' the count so you know when to change chords. If this is hard to understand then please go to the website and watch the video describing bars and how to deal with them.

There is so much music based on the 12-bar system. Blues, rock and roll, folk music and much popular music. Below is a 12-bar blues system. This is a nice easy way to represent it.

Each square in the diagram represents one bar. A bar is 4 beats. 1,2,3,4. Count it. 1,2,3,4.

Each line in the diagram represents four bars. And the number in the box means we play that note according to our 1-4-5 system.

So on the top line we play the keynote C for 4 bars (1,2,3,4 – four times).

On the second line we play the dominant F for two bars (two counts of 4), then the key C for two counts of 4.

And on the bottom line, one bar of (the subdominant) G, one bar of F, one bar of C, and one bar of G. The last bar of G is known as the turnaround.

It looks like this…

I 4 Beats of 1	I 4 Beats of 1	I 4 Beats of 1	I 4 Beats of 1
IV 4 Beats of 4	IV 4 Beats of 4	I 4 Beats of 1	I 4 Beats of 1
V 4 Beats of 5	IV 4 Beats of 4	I 4 Beats 1	V 4 Beats 5

You will notice this system only uses three chords; they may be Major, minor or a mix of both. There are also different variations on this system but this is it in its simplicity.

Key Learnings

- The blues can be played many ways
- It is as simple as adding the 7th to Major chords
- It can be a mix of Major and minor
- There is a common 12-bar system which is used in a lot of blues music

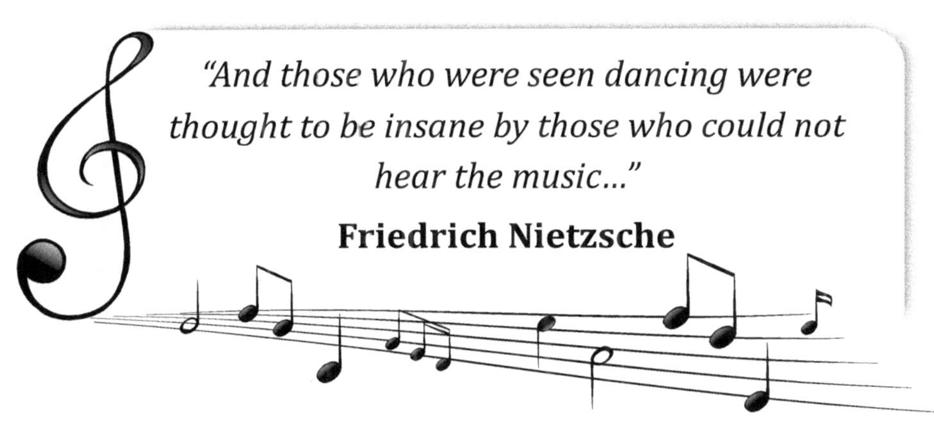
"And those who were seen dancing were thought to be insane by those who could not hear the music..."
Friedrich Nietzsche

Chord charts (and how to use them)

Some may think that playing your favourite songs when you don't read music may present a problem. Let me introduce you to chord charts. Chords are all identified by a system of symbols. Trouble is there are a number of symbols for each chord so any particular chord could be represented by four different symbols. Generally however Major chords are usually written as a single letter or sometimes with a capital M. Thus C or CM. (You will also notice that I have written Major with a capital 'M' throughout the book to emphasise its majorness and differentiate it from the minor.) You may also see Cmaj or Cma. Minor is usually written with a small m thus Cm or sometimes as a small c, cmin or cmi. But usually it's Cm. The same applies to any chord you may come across and some of them can get pretty unreal.

Below is a small example of a chord chart. This is just to show you how they are written and what you can expect from a chord chart. When learning a piece from a chord chart it is important to *go slowly and get a feel for it*. It can begin as simply as playing and holding the chord once and singing the words below it. As you play it a couple of times you will naturally come up to speed and include your own interpretation of the song. There are many songs that use only two or three chords and these are a good place to start. As my dad used to say, "Keep it simple stupid." Do yourself a favour and begin with something easy and work your way up to the more complex. The first song I could play and sing was 'Turn the Page' by Bob Seger and what a thrill it gave me when I got it. I have demonstrated how this works on the website so go and have a look at the video on using chord charts to learn a song. Below is a chord chart of the Beatles song – 'And I Love Her'.

AND I LOVE HER the Beatles

Em Bm

I give her all my love

Em Bm

That's all I do

Em Bm

And if you saw my love

G   A

You'd love her too

D

I love her

Unlike formally written music that tells you exactly how a piece of music 'should' be played, chord charts just give you the basics and it is up to you to interpret the music your way. So you have options when you play a piece from a chord chart depending on how you 'hear' it. We all have a memory of our favourite pieces and hit songs in our heads and so when learning to play a song from a chord chart those memories influence how we play it and make it sound. You also have the choice to play the chords as written or enhance them with 2nds, 4ths, 7ths and so on. Sometimes I will hear a tune (one that I have been playing) on the radio and realise I have strayed far from the original and that the way I hear it in my head is very different from the way the original artist played it.

This is normal and absolutely okay. Think of some of the cover versions of songs you have heard that you like. Mostly you will only play songs that you know and are familiar with from a chord chart. Occasionally I will play a song I have never heard from a chord chart. Depending on the song it can be difficult or easy. Try it one day and see what you come up with. Then go to YouTube and listen to the original. It is a very interesting exercise.

When starting out and beginning to learn a song such as the one above you need to play it very slowly. You can play and hold the chord, sing the lines, then play and hold the next chord. Continue to do this as you work your way through the song. Don't rush, get a 'feel' for the tune, listen to where the chord changes and enjoy the process. If you hit a chord you don't know stop and work it out before going on. (Note: sometimes you can skip a chord or play a normal chord instead of a 7th and it still sounds fine.) Gradually bring the song up to speed. Put inflections in. Play the chord quicker or finger each note in the chord.

Make it yours. Remember the same rule applies as in practice. If you make a mistake slow it down and play it slower a few times then bring it back up to speed. The other thing to know here is that a song will not always be in a key that you can sing. You will know immediately if this is the case as it will be difficult for you because it will either be too high or too low. If you are playing on a keyboard with a transpose button it is very easy to change it up or down to a key that suits you better. If not then you will have to change it yourself. This is not so difficult and one can get very good at reading one chord and playing a different one. Let me explain using the example above. To move the key *up one* in our example Em becomes Fm, Bm becomes Cm and G, A and D all become sharp – G#, A# and D#

Key Learnings

- Chord charts make learning songs easy without needing to 'read' music
- Play the song very slowly get a feel for it and build up to speed
- There are an untold number of chord charts available on the internet
- You may need to change the key for your vocal range. You can use the transpose button or just move it all up or down as you need

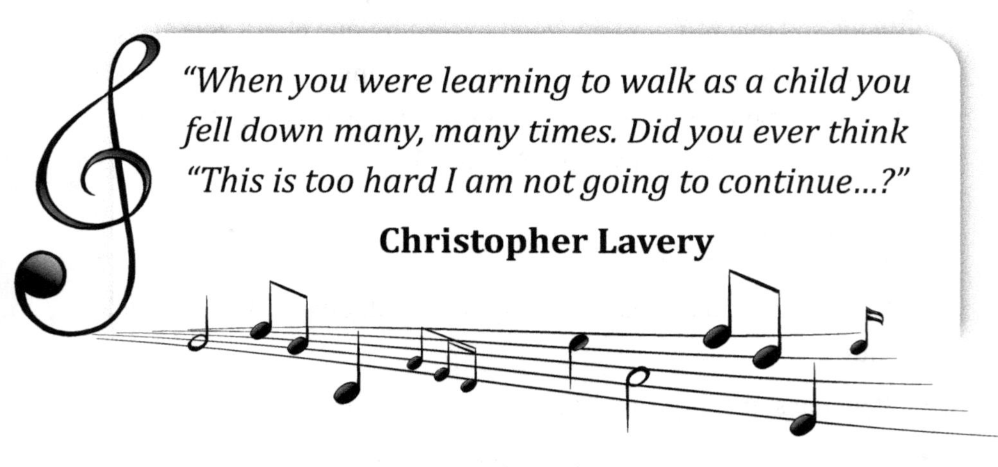
"When you were learning to walk as a child you fell down many, many times. Did you ever think "This is too hard I am not going to continue...?"
Christopher Lavery

Improvisation and jamming

If you have gotten this far into the book you already have all the tools you need to sit at the piano or pick up any other instrument and play to your heart's content without needing a piece of paper in front of you. You now also have the ability to play with others and enjoy jamming and creating new sounds.

I have given you the secret formula for chord progression, i.e. 1-4-5. You know or can work out the relative minor chords for any key and you know that you can add in any chord that fits with the 4 or the 5.

You have the key to working out any scale in any key. Want to play along with a bunch of blues musicians? Easy. It's just three chords played in progression. What key are they playing in? What is the 1-4-5 of that key? Mostly it will be A, C, D, E, F or G. Few musos venture into B or black key territory. Want to do a lead break? Then play the blues scale in the key they are jamming in. It's usually a 12-bar so you get 12 bars to do your thing and strut your stuff. The only way to learn is by doing, so don't worry about stuffing it up or looking silly. Everyone has to start somewhere.

This is the beautiful thing about a keyboard. You can set it up with auto accompaniment and jam along with yourself. I have provided some chord progressions on the website so you can download them to any audio device and play along.

Remember if you are jamming and improvising you are making it all up so the rules are relaxed and you can feel free to explore and create whatever you wish.

I like to spend part of my practice time improvising and exploring different chords and scales.

Sometimes I will explore the 'jazz modes' or something like the *eight-tone Spanish* scale. It is fun to learn new scales and see where they take you. Below are a couple of formulas for improvisation.

1. Find a scale you wish to explore
2. Choose a key
3. Play a chord or bass line with your left hand
4. Play the scale with your right hand
5. Using the 1-4-5 you can use three scales
6. For example, play a C chord, play the C scale. Move to F chord, play F scale. Move to G chord, play G scale, etc.
7. If you are playing another instrument like a saxophone you can mix up the three scales/chords and put something nice together using the 1-4-5 system
8. If you are on a keyboard or have rhythms available you can choose one to play with

And another

1. Choose a type of chord you wish to explore
2. Choose a key
3. Play chords with both hands or play bass keys with left
4. Play the chords in the 1-4-5 progression adding in other chords as you wish

There are no hard and fast rules to follow. That's the point. Use these as a guide and take it further. Explore. Music has a vast palette and unfortunately most of us are only using a small number of colours. Spread your wings.

Get jamming

At the age of 55 I began jamming with a few other people on a weekly basis which led me to being the lead singer in the band that came out of that. The guys I was jamming with were all older fellows who wanted to play music and have a bit of fun. We found each other through an ad one of them placed on the internet through an app called Gumtree, you may have heard of that? Two things I learned from the experience.

i) Playing music with others is a whole lot of fun. When you collaborate with a group of musicians something special happens. As you get into rapport with each other and allow your different styles to blossom and grow there is a creative energy that finds expression and manifests in some wonderful moments. I am forever grateful for the opportunity to play and create music with a bunch of wonderful people and I now know the love that band members have for each other (when you get the mix right). Fronting the band was an incredible experience and I was able to fulfil my childhood fantasies of being a rock star. We may not have been filling stadiums but we packed them into the clubs and pubs we played and we got 'em up dancing and having fun.

ii) My playing improved dramatically. As I now had to support others and do my bit the pressure was on. And as is the case we tend to perform better under a bit of pressure. (Too much leads to mental health problems but that is another story.) Whilst playing by and for yourself is great it allows you to make mistakes or take shortcuts that you cannot do when you are playing in a band and things need to be 'tight'. So I highly recommend playing with others as soon as possible. It took me far too long to do this with any regularity.

These days I regularly sing in public. Does everyone like my singing? Unlikely. There will always be people who dislike what you do, doesn't matter what that you do. The trick is not to be affected by those people and allow them to stop you. Often when I was performing on the street at festivals and the like I was confronted by people who didn't like what I was doing (I did camp it up a bit…okay a lot) and they would yell stuff like "Get a real job mate!" I used to inwardly chuckle as I knew how much I was making compared to the 'average' wage earner. Probably 20 years after becoming an entertainer one of my brothers asked me, not for the first time. "When are you going to stop all this clowning crap and get a real job?" So I gave him the only answer I knew he would understand and asked him, "Do you realise how much money I make?" When I told him his jaw dropped and he has never mentioned it again. I have found very few people really support you in what you want to do. When I first announced to the world that I was going to study performing arts (at the age of 30) there was not much support shown. Except for my mother, my family and friends laughed and made fun of me. (Time for some new friends?)

This was the very reason I stopped performing back in high school. It just wasn't 'cool' where I grew up to do stuff like that. Any man who liked dancing or acting had to be gay and if not was certainly suspected and was subject to howls of derision. Unfortunately I had gone from one school where there was a drama program and school plays to another where drama was non-existent and there *had* been no school plays until I had been there a few years. So when I signed up for the school musical in my final year my 'mates' made it their personal mission to give me such a hard time that I withdrew from the play and never looked at anything arty again until I reached that painful point in life where I just had to follow what life was calling me to do or be condemned to a life of misery. So please, don't allow others to dictate what you do and don't do in life.

Key Learnings

- If you really want something nothing should stop you
- Nothing improves your performance like regular (daily) practice
- Do not listen to what other people think YOU should do
- It is never too late to get started
- Finding others to jam with is not only a great deal of fun but it will lift your performance and accelerate your learning

"It never seems to occur to people that a man might just want to write a piece of music..."
Ralph Vaughan Williams

Songwriting

One of the most pleasurable things I have ever done is writing a song. There is something incredibly exciting and satisfying about putting words and music together. I never thought I would know how to do this but through consistent practice these skills emerge. Many people think only special people with special talent can write songs. I know I did. We hold the songwriters in high esteem, marvel at their skill and award them special prizes and accolades for the pleasure they bring us. The reality is that like most things in life there is a system and when you know the system you too can be successful.

There are two parts to writing a song; the lyrics and the music. Some people find the music first and then put words to it, others find the words first and then put music to them. There is no right way to do it but essentially people like to tell a story. Blues artists tell of hard times, Country musicians tell of life on the land, folk musicians may put poetry to music and others sing songs of joy and love. Essentially lyrics tell a story and the story can be told many ways. Verse or prose? Chorus no chorus? How you do it is up to you. Lyrics often contain a *hook*. A hook is a phrase or word that *hooks* a listener into the song just as a hook grabs a fish and reels them in. Often the hook is also the title of the song and is the purpose and reason for writing the song.

People have been singing and chanting for as long as we know. The voice is presumed to be the original musical instrument and as far as we know there is no human culture regardless of how remote or isolated that does not sing. Singing is fundamental to who we are. We have always been singers and will remain so as long as we communicate through using the larynx.

Most modern songs have an introduction, verses and a chorus.

When it comes to constructing the music part of the song you can of course use any key, any scales and any chords you like. However there is a reason so many songs use the 1-4-5 system and that is because most of us agree it sounds *good.* Many songs have been written using only these three chords. We can also add the relative minor chord to the mix. Lots of popular songs use this relative minor chord. It provides a change in the sound yet also sounds 'right' in the 1-4-5 mix. So great, there is our four chord song in a nutshell and for sure you can go ahead, as many already have, and use these four chords with much success. (Some have successfully written good songs using just one chord, notably Bo Diddley, Chuck Berry and many bluesmen.) This is all you need to write songs that will sound good and be appreciated. Remember my Dad's advice. *"Keep it simple stupid."* Good so far?

Let's have a look at the most common structure of songs.

Introduction

Verse

Chorus

Verse

Chorus

Bridge

Chorus

Outro

Not all of the above parts have to be used in a song. Many simply use verse–chorus–verse–chorus. Others will use a bridge, some include instrumentals, others don't and introductions and outros are all used at the song writer's discretion. I suggest you look at songs you like and use the structures you find pleasing.

If you're looking to take it further and want more? How can we expand on those four chords and make the song more 'interesting' while still keeping it sounding 'good'?

Let's take another look at the 1-4-5 pattern.

We have number one (the keynote), number four (the subdominant) and number five (the dominant). And we added the relative minor (down three from the keynote). What if we take the 1-4-5 pattern and apply it to the dominant and the subdominant note? So using our example of C-F-G what if we included the chords that appear on the F and the G. In other words think of the F and the G as your keynote or number one. That then gives us C-F-G plus the chords on the F which is F-A-C plus the chords built on the G which gives us G-B-D and the relative minors of the F and G, Dm and Em. And don't forget the 1-4-5 can be Major or minor which expands it even further.

Of course there is no reason you have to stick with Major and minor chords. Why not play with other chords? There are lots to choose from on our chord charts? You *could* use suspended, augmented or diminished chords without too much trouble or be bold and try some of the dozens of other chords available.

Now we have an expanded song writing palette of ten chords we can use knowing that these ten chords will fit and sound good in the mix. Observant people will notice we have actually covered all the notes A to G so really it depends where and how we use any particular chord in a song and what formula we use when we are putting that song together.

There is a whole other book just on the subject of song writing so I am not going to go into too much depth here. I just want you to know that you too can put a song together.

Key Learnings

- Song writing is very satisfying
- There are formulas for writing songs
- We have agreements about what sounds good
- Songwriters use hooks to get you in
- Songs are essentially a story or poem put to music
- See The Understanding of Songwriting Seminar

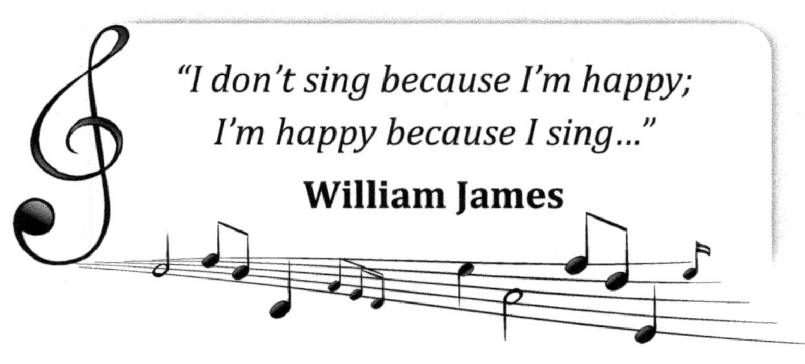
*"I don't sing because I'm happy;
I'm happy because I sing..."*
William James

Singing

"Can you whistle? Cause you can't sing." This is a phrase I heard often as I grew up, from friends, older brothers (are all older brothers complete bastards, is there something in the older brother handbook that says one must be cruel to younger brothers?) and even complete strangers. And it is a major reason why many people are scared of singing. It is a favourite put-down designed to get a laugh but it is always at someone's expense. Maybe yours? If you have ever had someone have a go at you when you were singing and it now affects you then you would do well to find a way to let it go and just sing.

Many famous singers would tell you they have terrible voices and yet they have enjoyed fabulous success. Look at the careers of people like Rod Stewart, a raspy gravelling voice if ever there was one. Joe Cocker? Sweet voice? No way! I am sure you can think of many others. I learned early on in my career as an entertainer that I don't have to be *the best*; I just have to know that I am *good enough* and that people (not all) will enjoy what I offer.

Once I stopped comparing myself with the best in my field and compared myself instead to the 99% of the population who were not doing what I do, those who were leading 'average' lives doing 'average' things then I was able to go forward feeling empowered and confident.

As William James says in the quote at the beginning of this chapter, *"I don't sing because I am happy, I am happy because I sing."*

***Singing is good for you*!**

It gets you breathing deeply, it gets your blood circulation, it stirs the emotions, and it is uplifting. One of the best teachers I ever had was Mr Jacobs, my Year 6 teacher. Every morning Mr Jacobs would begin his classes by pulling out the tuning fork and making us do singing exercises. He would bang his tuning fork on the desk and get it humming then cajole and demand that we all "sing C". He was an old school type with a military background and it put everyone in the mood for the more formal lessons that were to come throughout the day. He knew the power of singing.

Why are TV shows like *The Voice* so popular? People love hearing someone sing well. It stirs us. It moves us, and makes us feel good.

For many years I worked at many annual local Carols by Candlelight events and was always amazed how popular they were. People turned out in their tens of thousands for a chance to sing along with all the other people from their community, the choir and the lead vocalists.

Have you ever attended a performance by the Welsh mens' choir, or the Vienna boys' choir or perhaps your local church choir? No one leaves untouched. I can assure you the members of the choir feel it even more so. Singing in a choir or with a group of other people creates a feeling of joy and bliss. How many ways can I say it? Singing is good for your health, physically, mentally and spiritually. And yet we shy away from it and put others down for doing it in public?

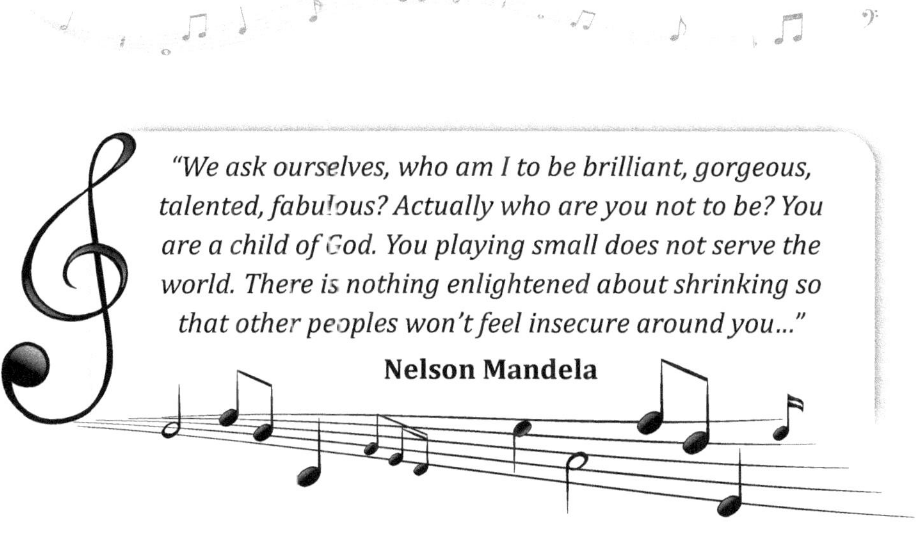

I believe, given the chance and the encouragement…

There are very few people who can't sing

Everybody has a voice. It may not be a *great* voice but it is *good enough*. If I asked you to hum a few lines of your favourite song, I am sure you could do so perfectly. All of us have listened to thousands of hours of music. It is everywhere. On the radio. In the car. At the shopping centre. In elevators, waiting rooms, at markets and special events. We celebrate music everywhere. Concerts, festivals, records, CDs, tapes, smartphones, MP3 players. We cannot get enough music.

As long as someone else is playing and singing. People that apparently have some special ability that is beyond the rest of us?

These are great excuses for not having a go or for staving off the possible embarrassment of singing in public and risking the kind of ridicule we started this chapter with.

Do you think when we were living in villages and gathering around the campfires that some of us weren't allowed to sing? That we were considered not good enough? I don't think so. It is just like in ancient Greece where everyone played multiple instruments, in times gone by everybody enjoyed singing. We must get over the fear that is so endemic in our modern world. Singing is a joy and a gift to be enjoyed and practiced by all.

It makes me sad that so many of us never realise our potential in so many areas of our lives. We stay safe and play a very small game, not allowing ourselves to take on tasks that would greatly enrich our lives and give meaning and purpose. Not to mention the contribution you could make to the world.

I lost count of the number of times I had students say to me when I was running juggling workshops, "Oh I am unco" (Aussie slang for unco-ordinated) when they weren't uncoordinated at all. They were just scared to fail, too lazy to put in the effort or scared of looking foolish in front of their peers. What a tragedy to go through life afraid to have a go, too timid to try, or worried what others may think.

The most valuable mathematical equations I have ever learned look like this…

Input = Output

Meaning you will only get out of something what you are prepared to put in. When it comes to music you will only be as good as the amount of time you have spent practicing. Those artists you see and hear that you love and admire have probably put in thousands of hours practicing their craft. Talent usually equals a whole lot of hard work

Output = Input

Conversely in order to get things flowing your way you need to be outputting. If you want to get a job for instance, you need to be out there looking, putting in your resume and applying for positions. The more you *do* so the more likely it is you *will* succeed.

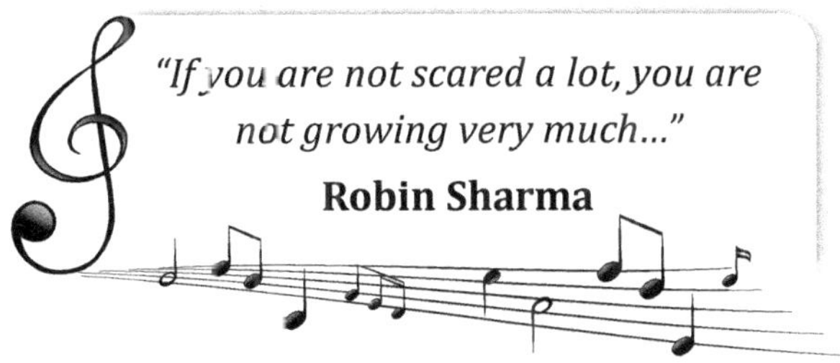

Here are two good ways to practise your singing. As with practising your musical instrument you can lock yourself away in a room so no one else can hear (and comment) or you can join a choir where you can hide in amongst a multitude of voices and enjoy the thrill of singing with a bunch of other people. It is incredibly uplifting to sing in a choir and you will improve your own singing and enjoy the company of others while doing so. I began singing when I was performing with a cabaret act called The Sophistocatz. I was doing the comedy juggling and fire-eating and the singers wanted me to come on stage for our finale and join them in song.

No one kicked me off stage or told me to just mouth the words because I was terrible, so that gave me the confidence to find and attend an a cappella (no music) course being run at the local community college. From there I began scouring the web for midi files and backing tracks to songs I liked and I began to sing along with them. At that stage I wasn't playing the keyboard at all.

Later when I had been playing for some years, I was able to download chord charts and sing along to my own playing. I was so thrilled when I learned to play and sing my first song. I couldn't believe I could actually play and sing. I had always admired others who had this 'talent' (and a little envious) and now I could do it as well. Wow! I was so thrilled, chuffed and proud of myself.

Here's the thing… ***If I can do it, so can you!***

I have had no formal singing lessons. I have always enjoyed singing. I liked it at school, I liked it around the campfire, I liked it in the car on long drives. So it seemed a natural progression to sing along with playing the keyboard. There came a point when I wanted to learn some tunes and I wanted to sing along with them. When it comes to singing I do have the magical ingredient I have told you about previously and that is I am a very persistent and I have learned *not to listen to others*. For the most part I have locked myself away and practiced in private, only being heard by my amazing wife Natascha. And I do not exaggerate when I tell you she was in tears at times asking me to please stop. (Not so much because my voice was so bad but because I had a habit of playing blues and sad songs first thing in the morning.) I knew though that I was improving, that I *was* getting better all the time and that even if no one else was enjoying it, *I* certainly was. I knew I had had a breakthrough when one day Natascha came and opened the door and said she (and others) wanted to hear me practise.

There is a little secret I will share with you here and that is, when a vocalist is singing into a microphone their voice is going through a sound FX system and at the very least is adding what is called *reverb* to their voice. Reverb is a shortening on the word reverberation which means, "*A prolongation of a sound or a resonance.*" This effect makes the voice sound richer, fuller and just better than if there was no effect at all. The reason many people enjoy singing in the shower is because of the reverberation effect of singing in that enclosed space. It is the echoing and repeating effect that makes it sound so good. Singers singing from stage use these effects electronically to make their voices sound better than they would otherwise.

In the digital age it is possible to run your voice through a computer that will enhance anything you sing and make it impossible to be off-key or sound anything but wonderful. When was the last time you heard a bad singer on a TV talent show? It is just amazing how many incredible voices are out there. Such an abundance of talent on show to make the rest of us feel totally inadequate. If you are of my generation you will remember *bad* singers on TV talent shows, people who were off-key and struggled with high notes. If you are under 30, ask your parents or grandparents.

If you are not confident with your singing there is help at hand. Freeing the voice from the constraints that have built up over a lifetime of being told *you are not good enough* is a process like any other. Getting help is possibly the fastest route. This can take many forms. Yoga, breath work, hypnotism or a vocal coach. There are many ways to free yourself and find your true authentic voice. All you really need is a desire and a determination to free yourself. *When the student is ready the teacher shall appear.* This is an ancient saying attributed to the likes of Buddha and Confucius. Its origin is lost in time but the truth of this saying has proven itself to me many times.

The first thing to learn when you put yourself in the public eye is how to be relaxed and comfortable. You need to be confident that they cannot harm you in any way. This is why people practise and rehearse in private, sometimes for years, so that they have the confidence in their ability to front an audience and be well received. No one wants to flop. Is it worth the effort? Yes, yes, yes, a resounding yes.

You may recall Susan Boyle? Susan was the winner of the TV show *Britain's Got Talent*. She came onto the show a dowdy, poorly groomed middle aged woman who immediately copped the derision of the judges and the audience, just for the way she looked. But – she was feisty, and more than that, she was ready. Susan had spent years of her life singing to local people from her village, she enjoyed singing for its own sake and had reached a top-class standard. No one her own circle knew who she was. She had worked away in private. Others from her village had convinced her she was good enough and watching her before her performance, when she was being questioned by the judges, it certainly looked like she knew how good she was. And boy oh boy did her life change when she came out. Is it worth it? Hell yeah. No effort goes unrewarded. But also, no-effort goes unrewarded.

Put in the effort – reap the reward.
Put in no effort – receive no reward.

Key Learnings

- Singing is good for your health
- Singing, or the belief that one can sing, seems to have been beaten out of most of us
- There is lots of growth, satisfaction and confidence to be gained by singing (in public)
- Everyone can sing, we have just been suppressed and brainwashed into thinking we can't

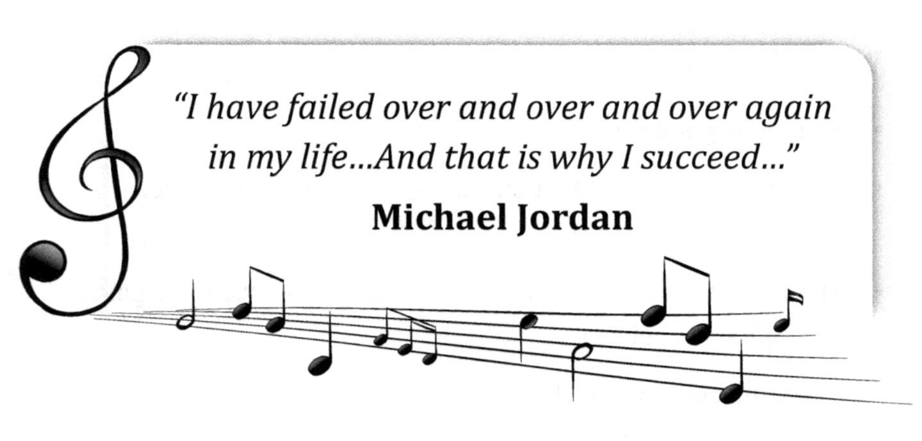
"I have failed over and over and over again in my life...And that is why I succeed..."
Michael Jordan

The amazing modern electronic keyboard

Okay. I know this book is called *Piano and Keyboard Made Easy* and everything I have given you applies to the piano but I love keyboards. Modern keyboards are incredible. Even the cheapest children's keyboards usually have hundreds of different rhythms and hundreds of different tones. You literally have the musical world at your fingertips. Pop and rock, ballads, dance, swing, jazz, rhythm and blues, country, Latin, ballroom, and lots, lots, more.

The keyboard with its abundance of styles becomes your teacher. Would you like to learn different styles? Then look no further. An electronic keyboard can teach you. Many musicians become stuck only knowing a few particular styles. They learn from their teachers, peers or whoever they can, and so are limited, like my concert pianist friend who wished to play blues but had no idea how. When it comes to tones there are heaps of different piano sounds, electric pianos, strings, orchestral instruments, guitars and basses, saxophones, flutes and woodwind, organs, trumpets and many types of brass, harmonicas, accordions, human voices, sound effects and percussion and drum kits. Learn the keyboard and you can play any of these instruments to a high standard. And if that is not enough for you many have USB slots so you can plug in as many more as you like. Some keyboards connect directly to the internet and you can download songs, lessons,

rhythms and other very useful information. And far from the thin tinny sounds of days gone by modern samples of the instruments are incredibly realistic. Of course the more expensive the instrument the better quality the sound gets.

You can use the built-in speakers or plug in to an external amplifier and really get rocking. Of course practising in private is highly recommended and a keyboard makes it easy by simply plugging in a set of headphones. Nobody else has to hear your mistakes and experimentation and you can quickly learn and please yourself. Remember, when you first set out you are doing it for yourself. When you become accomplished, then you can share it for others to enjoy.

Many keyboards also offer built-in recording and the ability to plug in a microphone and use special built in vocal effects. My keyboards allow me to have full backing from the built in rhythms, a range of instruments at my fingertips and produce a three- or four-part harmony with my vocals. It is amazing. I can also plug into my computer for recording and include an amazing array of special effects and vocal layering. What a time to be alive. Can you imagine if Beethoven had such things available to him what he may have done with it?

One thing I need to mention is that different brands of keyboard use different systems and it can be challenging going from one brand to another. For some years now I have only used Yamaha keyboards as I like their system and have become used to using it. I have in the past owned Casio and Roland keyboards and they were wonderful keyboards but for me I prefer and stick to using Yamaha keyboards.

I want to show you a few different levels of keyboard so you can see there is something for every budget and every level of expertise. You can start with a Yamaha PSR-F50. It is about as basic as it gets and a great starter keyboard, especially for children. It is small and light, has a regular size keyboard and packs in 120 voices and 114 rhythms. All this, for under AUS$150 brand new, much less on the second-hand market. For this money you may not get *all* the features I spoke of above but this is a great place to start if you have never owned a keyboard and cost is a consideration. It will give you hours of pleasure and whet your appetite for something with more features and more power.

Jump up a little to something like the Yamaha PSR-E453. It is still basic, inexpensive, and simple and yet it is incredibly powerful. It has 768 different voices available and over 200 different rhythms to choose from. You also get USB connectivity, higher quality voices and rhythms and a whole bunch of other features like *touch sensitive keys*. You can plug it into external devices like a laptop or iPad which opens up a whole world of possibilities. And it is available brand new for less than AUS$500. Bargain!

I recommend buying a keyboard with ***touch sensitive keys****. This allows you to moderate your volume simply by the pressure you place on a key, much like it does when you play a 'real' piano.*

My favourite the Yamaha PSR-S950. Ain't nothing it can't do. I have used Yamaha products for some years now and stick to them as I know the Yamaha system and love what they can do. I have found them to be robust and long lasting and they are capable of doing things I cannot even imagine. When it comes to reading manuals I am a skimmer. I read what I need, when I need to know it, and then toss it in a drawer and forget about it. I also have a PSR-3000 that I have had for years and I still use and love. It has been dragged and bumped all over the place for jams and gigs and never misses a beat. I bought the PSR-S950 about two years ago and am really enjoying its amazing sound quality. Guitars sound like guitars, including fret noises; brass instruments sound incredibly real; saxophones are amazing and there is a huge range of different electric piano and organ sounds to choose from. I love playing with the drum kits and of course I plug a microphone through the keyboard and use the many vocal effects available including, three- and four-part harmonies that the keyboard creates. It is incredible. It is a love affair. As you become a better player you'll want one. Yours for around AUS$2000.

When you dial in a rhythm you like (or press a couple of buttons) and press the ACMP (accompaniment) button on your keyboard you will be offered multiple introductions and endings, a choice of different styles within the rhythm and one-touch settings and registrations. When you find one you like create a registration so you can go back to it any time. This does involve reading your manual and working out how to do that but is very worth the effort. The modern keyboard is truly an absolute marvel. What a sad state of affairs it is that so few people actually know how to use it properly. I wish to teach you exactly how to use the modern keyboard in a way that is effective and really enjoyable. Once you have got your head and fingers around the 1-4-5 system you can sit down and play your favourite tunes or improvise to your heart's content.

Please go to the website and watch the video on how to use the ACMP properly. You can very quickly and very easily sound like a pro. Want to play blues? Simple. Dial up your favourite blues style, press the ACMP button and start with a favourite chord. You may like to use the auto-chord or one finger chord section on the lower part of the keyboard or make the whole keyboard responsive by moving the split point all the way to the right hand side so that no matter where you play a chord you will sound good.

Styles have different applications and they're very useful depending on what you want to do. My PSR-S950 gives me three different introductions, four main variations of the rhythm, a break button and three different endings. I also get up to eight different lead instruments. What a lot of possibilities. Did I mention I can also plug a microphone directly into the keyboard and I can use the built in vocal effects? This allows me to have a three- or four-part backing vocals, in male or female voices, various different FX imposed on my own voice and I can even change my voice into a female voice. Crazy, man! For more on how to do this go to the website and check out the videos in the keyboard section.

Yamaha offers the range topping Yamaha Tyros5. (Yes that means there are four previous versions on the second hand market.

The Tyros is the ultimate in keyboards. It does everything that can be done on a keyboard and it does it using the latest technology and the best samplings available. The sound is incredible and the array of voices, instruments and rhythms at your fingertips is unbelievable. For mine I find it a bit large and cumbersome for gigs but at home in the studio it is awesome.

Key Learnings

- Modern keyboards are incredible
- A keyboard will teach you to play in any style
- A keyboard will give you full backing for you to play and sing
- You can create special FX and personalised sounds
- You can use multiple instruments
- For more information on keyboards and how to use them visit the website

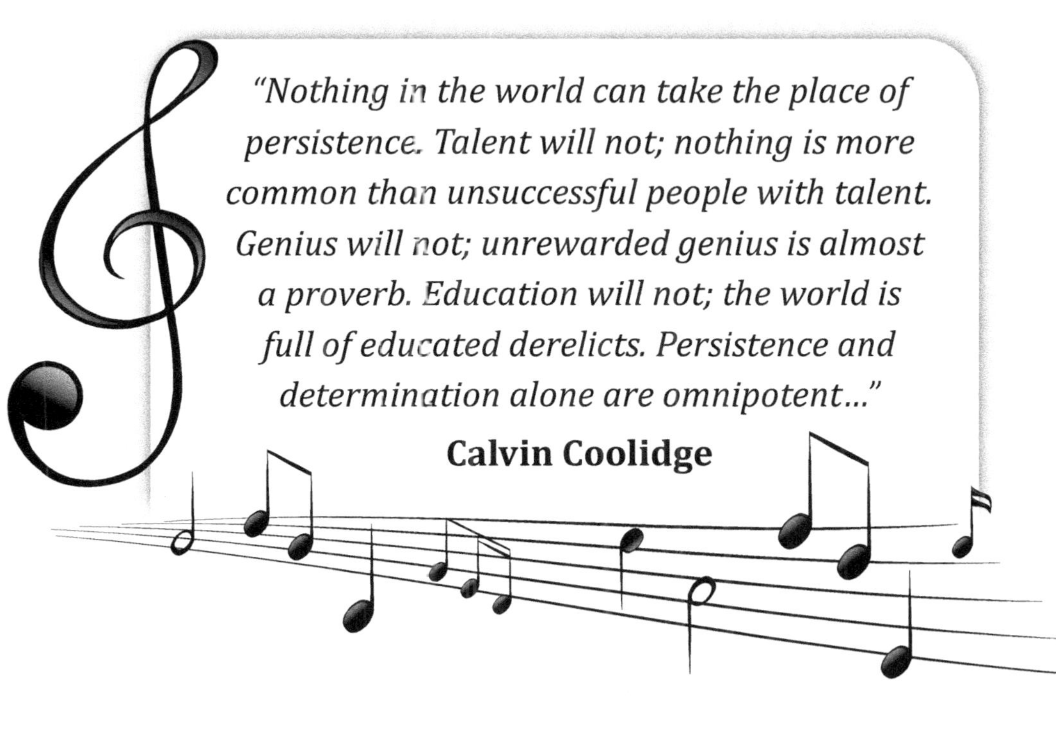
"Nothing in the world can take the place of
persistence. Talent will not; nothing is more
common than unsuccessful people with talent.
Genius will not; unrewarded genius is almost
a proverb. Education will not; the world is
full of educated derelicts. Persistence and
determination alone are omnipotent..."
Calvin Coolidge

Don't let others stop you

Strange as it seems, those around you don't want you to change, learn new skills, stop bad habits or become different in any way. They like you just the way you are. (Unless you are a massive pain in the backside, then they just wish you would go and annoy someone else.) Try to stop smoking, attempt to lose weight, change career, whatever it is, those around you are not always super encouraging. And in fact they can be downright discouraging. It may be they fear you will have less time for them. They might be frightened they will have to change too. It just might bring up their own fears and inadequacies. Regardless of their reasons you need to be aware you may find resistance to you learning music and playing an instrument. So brace yourself.

When I decided to become a performing artist and study Performing Arts (at the age of 30) I was met with a lot of resistance. I got lots of comments like… "Are you crazy? What do you think you're doing?" And, "Is everything ok?" There was absolutely zero support for me going to study Performing Arts. Except from Mum. Because Mum sort of has to support you no matter what crazy scheme you may dream up.

Interestingly when I started to play saxophone and clarinet in my act, people I knew (who had failed in their attempts to play an instrument) would say things like you must have had the talent all the time. It was just lying there dormant waiting to be awakened and now it's come out. They couldn't accept that I had simply worked hard and become good at my music by practising daily. I have found this right through my career as a performing artist… "Aren't you amazing?!" "Oh, you are so talented." Yes, I have learned some amazing skills. I am a reasonably good juggler; I have good skills with the devil-sticks and diabolo. I can make good balloon animals, eat and twirl fire, perform on stilts and create good comedy characters. And I am an accomplished musician and singer. All of this has happened because of my willingness to push though barriers and work hard and a refusal to give up.

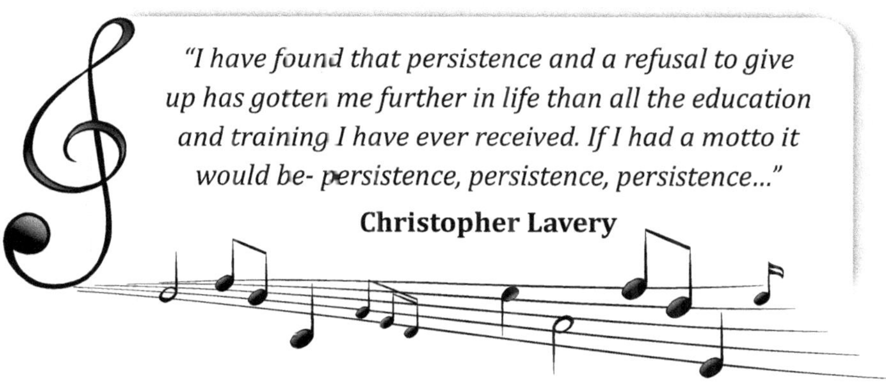

Develop 'good' habits and be disciplined

No, sorry. It is not about talent! At least, not for me. There may be people in this world who are born with amazing talent but I don't think I am one of them. What I am is stubborn. And persistent. And I have developed discipline and a willingness to practice daily even, if it's only for a few minutes. People don't realise the incredible benefits of doing something every day.

Think about something in your life that you are passionate about and have become good at. Chances are you have done it a lot and you have done it consistently. Whether that be sport, knitting, video games or riding a bicycle. I remember seeing the great motivational speaker E. James Rohn on stage in Melbourne. Jim asked the question. "If an apple a day really does keep the doctor away why don't we do it?" Answer: "Because it is easier not to."

I find it very easy to do (at least) ten push-ups and ten sit-ups and a few stretches when I get out of bed in the morning. Ten a day equals 3650 per year. Would that help most people's strength and do good things for your health? Probably would, but most people won't do these simple little things that can give great benefit over the long term. Learning an instrument is the same; small amounts of time add up to incredible benefits and joy in the long term. So please develop the discipline to take on tasks you know you would like and/or will give you great benefits. Learn to 'chunk' your time on different things throughout the day and you will become an expert in many things.

So this is just a little warning for anyone contemplating taking up music or doing anything else different. Your friends and family, your acquaintances and work colleagues will quite often be discouraging to the new thing or the change in you that they are seeing. Unless you are surrounded by an incredibly supporting and loving bunch you may find that the people around you don't want you to change. If you take up an instrument and start getting good at it, you will change. You will see the world differently. You will see yourself differently.

Generally the people around you do not want you to grow and change because it makes them feel insecure and uncomfortable.

Key Learnings

- People will try to stop you. They like you *just* the way you are
- It's not about talent
- Work and persistence will get you a long way
- You are the sum of your habits

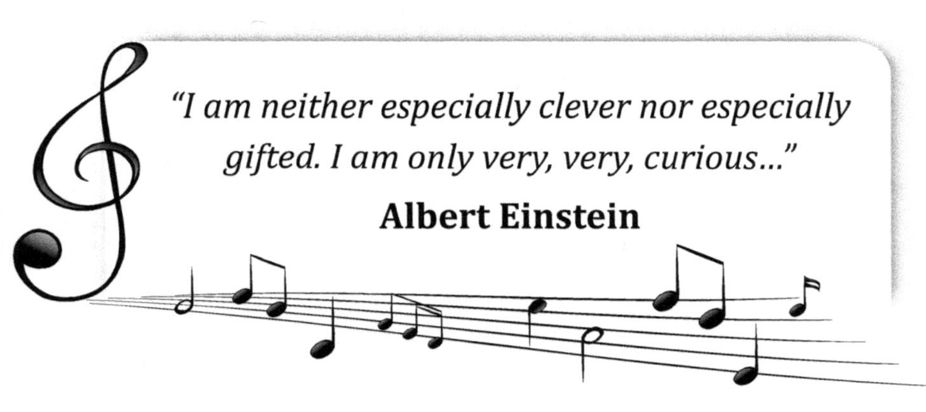
"I am neither especially clever nor especially gifted. I am only very, very, curious..."
Albert Einstein

Epilogue

My parting message to all budding musicians and all people wishing to grow and prosper in life is this…

A very wise person once told me that the quality of your self-talk determines the quality of your life and everything you do and achieve. As such the two most important words that you say to yourself are…

"I am."

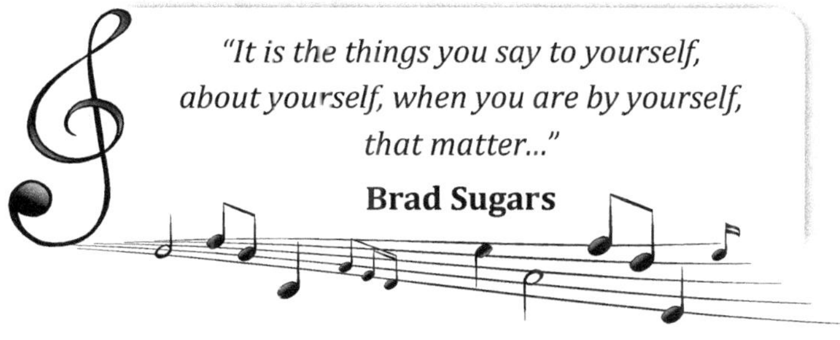

When you start a sentence in your head with "I am," pay close attention to the words that follow.

What do you say to yourself, about yourself when you are by yourself? Is it positive, self – affirming and loving? Or is it putting you down and implying you are not good enough?

"I am… what?"

In writing this book I have had to change my self-talk from, "Who do you think you are to be thinking you can write a book on music?" to "*I am* an author." It really started to become real for me when I got the cover designs back from the graphic artist. OMG! This is real. I am going to publish a book. Funny how the cover makes it more real than the tens of thousands of words that I had already written.

It has been an amazing journey putting down all these words. Modern technology makes it easier than ever for us to become authors. Most of this book was completed in the early hours of the day when I would sit down with a cuppa and speak into my smartphone. As I said previously. "What a time to be alive!" They say everyone has at least one book in them. Why not get yours out of your head and onto the bookshelves? Who knows who you might help and what impact you might have on the world?

My sincere hope is that these pages will help you if you are someone who has always wanted to play an instrument but never got the opportunity, didn't know where to start or felt it was in the *too hard* basket. If you have been playing for a while and struggling to find a way through the maze of confusion that is music then I hope I have parted the curtains a little and given you a glimpse into its simplicity.

In writing the book I was torn between writing a textbook on music or putting music into the text of my life and revealing my journey. I feel that the journey I have taken may be inspiring to some of you and may help you find your own true path in life and music.

EPILOGUE

One thing is for sure; music is an inextricable part of my life and who I am. I play every day and if I don't, I start to get edgy and nervous. If I am away on holidays I go looking for pianos in hotel lobbies that I can play. I am addicted and obsessed and it is a love affair I will nourish and cherish until the day I die. Because of music I think differently and I act differently.

They say ignorance is bliss. And it can be bliss. It is incredibly frustrating if you have knowledge of something but are powerless to implement or affect anything with that knowledge. Knowledge is also bliss; when you can use that knowledge in ways that enhance and elevate your own and others life experience.

I urge you to use the knowledge you now have. Build the habit of music in your life. Spend the time learning an instrument, whether that is piano, keyboard or any other instrument. The rewards far outweigh any time and effort you put in. And seriously, *please* contact me if you have any questions or concerns. I am on a mission to help you find your musical pathway and I will answer.

Love & peace… March 2017

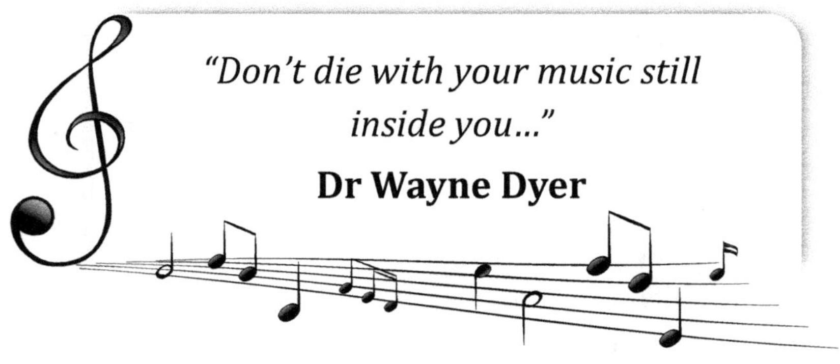
"Don't die with your music still
inside you..."
Dr Wayne Dyer

About the Author

Christopher Lavery

Christopher is an enthusiastic student of life and loves nothing more than a challenge. His life purpose is to inspire and motivate people to be, do and have more. More achievement, more abundance and more satisfaction and happiness. As well as being a self-taught musician he has mastered the art of juggling, fire eating, stilt-walking and public speaking.

He loves to travel and is available to speak to groups on the art of achievement and finding your genius.

If you would like Christopher to speak to your group he can be contacted through email at chris@pianoandkeyboardmadeeasy.com

RESOURCES

Recommended Resources

www.PianoAndKeyboardMadeEasy.com

For video explanations of the concepts in this book

www.understandingofmusic.com

The Understanding of Music Seminar™

www.ultimate-guitar.com

Guitar is played in the same pitch (i.e. 'C' or concert pitch) as piano and keyboard and so the chords are interchangeable on both instruments. This is a great site for finding songs and chords.

www.chordie.com

Another great site for finding chord charts.

"Teach your children well..."

Crosby, Stills & Nash

If you really want to help your children get them into music. Below is a list of benefits from the National Association for Music Education.

11 facts about music and children:

1. Children who study music tend to have larger vocabularies and more advanced reading skills than their peers who do not participate in music.

2. Children with learning disabilities or dyslexia who tend to lose focus with more noise could benefit greatly from music lessons.

3. Music programs are constantly in danger of being cut from shrinking school budgets even though they're proven to improve academics.

4. Children who study a musical instrument are more likely to excel in all of their studies, work better in teams, have enhanced critical thinking skills, stay in school, and pursue further education.

5. In the past, secondary students who participated in a music group at school reported the lowest lifetime and current use of all substances (tobacco, alcohol, and illicit drugs).

6. Schools with music programs have an estimated 90.2% graduation rate and 93.9% attendance rate compared to schools without music education, which average 72.9% graduation and 84.9% attendance.

7. Regardless of socioeconomic status or school district, students (3rd graders) who participate in high-quality music programs score higher on reading and spelling tests.

8. A Stanford study shows that music engages areas of the brain which are involved with paying attention, making predictions and updating events in our memory.

9. Much like expert technical skills, mastery in arts and humanities is closely correlated to a greater understanding of language components

10. Young children who take music lessons show different brain development and improved memory over the course of a year, compared to children who do not receive musical training.

11. Schools that have music programs have an attendance rate on 93.3% compared to 84.9% in schools without music programs.

www.ingramcontent.com/pod-product-compliance
Lightning Source LLC
Chambersburg PA
CBHW072006090426
42740CB00011B/2105
* 9 7 8 1 9 2 5 2 8 8 5 5 1 *